Also by Jane English

Tao Te Ching, by Lao Tsu, translation by Gia-fu Feng and Jane English, New York, Knopf/Vintage, 1972.

Inner Chapters, by Chuang Tsu, translation by Gia-fu Feng and Jane English, New York, Knopf/Vintage, 1974.

Waterchild, poetry by Judith Bolinger, photographs by Jane English, London/Pomona, Wildwood House/Hunter House, 1980.

Accept This Gift: Selections from A Course in Miracles, Walsh and Vaughan, editors, Los Angeles, Tarcher, 1983. (Illustrated with photographs by Jane English.)

Different Doorway
Adventures of a Caesarean Born

by
Jane Butterfield English

EARTH HEART • Point Reyes Station • California

Earth Heart
P. O. Box 1027
Point Reyes Station, CA 94956

Editing: Jo Imlay & Cynthia Frank
Typesetting: Cynthia Frank & John Fremont—Comp-Type, Fort Bragg, CA.
Design: Chuck Hathaway—Mendocino Graphics, Fort Bragg, CA.
Printing: Skillful Means Press—Oakland, CA.

Acknowledgements to the following for generously granting permission for quotes and reproductions:
To Maxwell-Aley Associates for the quote from *The Brain Revolution* quoted in the February 13, 1972 journal entry.
To Parents Place, of Jewish Family and Children's Services, San Francisco for material from the May/June 1979 issue of their newsletter, "Offspring," quoted in the June 2, 1979 journal entry.
To The Mansell Collection, London, England for the Hieronymus Bosch painting used as Figure 14b.
To Rosemary Hayes for paintings used as Figures 15 through 19.
To Nancy Rosser-Hutchins for her drawing used as Figure 20.
To John Henze for the photograph of the author.

(All other paintings, drawings, and photographs are by the author.)

Library of Congress Cataloging in Publication Data
English, Jane Butterfield
  Different Doorway
  Adventures of a Caesarean Born
  Bibliography: p. 140
  1. English, Jane. 2. Cesarean birth—Psychological aspects.
3. Cesarean birth—Social aspects. 4. Cesarean birth—Spiritual aspects
5. Consciousness. 6. Mind and body. I. Title.
RG761.E54 1985   362.1'9886   85-80840
ISBN 0-934747-38-5
ISBN 0-934747-39-3 (pbk.)

DEDICATION

To my mother

On childhood walks in the woods, she led me off the beaten path in search of small adventures. She also insisted I learn to climb mountains.

Much of what I learned then I now see as basic training for the inner adventuring that has led to my writing this book.

List of Illustrations

Figure 1	Pink Teddy	22
Figure 2	The Well	29
Figure 3	The Ether Demon	30
Figure 4a	The Pregnant Castle	32
Figure 4b	The Castle Opening	33
Figure 5	Baseball Dream	34
Figure 6	Female Demon Dream	37
Figure 7	Boston Dream	49
Figure 8	Bottle Dream	53
Figure 9	Lighted Shadows	54
Figure 10	"This is Caesarean Birth" Dream	56
Figure 11	Birth Poem Photograph	62
Figure 12	Joint Jane Dream	65
Figure 13	Initiation Dream	66
Figure 14a	Falling into Physical Form ("The Well" by Jane English)	67
Figure 14b	Floating out of Physical Form ("Ascent to the Empyrean" by Hieronymus Bosch)	67
Figure 15	The Wound (by Rosemary Hayes)	106
Figure 16	The Firebird (by Rosemary Hayes)	108
Figure 17	Butterfly (by Rosemary Hayes)	109
Figure 18	Fire Tree (by Rosemary Hayes)	110
Figure 19	Buddha (by Rosemary Hayes)	111
Figure 20	Lifted Out With Love (by Nancy Rosser-Hutchins)	124
Figure 21a	Apples	137
Figure 21b	Apples and Banana	137

Table of Contents

Foreword—Stanislav Grof, M.D., Ph.D.   1

Prologue—Being at a Caesarean Delivery   3

Part I—The Territory   7

    "Caesarean Born" as a Conceptual Tool   8
    Inner Exploration   9
    Reality   10
    The Story   11

Part II—The Journey   15

    Chapter 1—Fire: Initiation   17
    Chapter 2—Water: Inner Depths   19
    Chapter 3—Air: Ideas and More Adventures   39
    Chapter 4—Seeds of Transformation   51
    Chapter 5—Earth: Transformation and Healing   71

Part III—Fellow Travelers   89

    Marilee James King—caesarean born therapist   90
    Natalie Ednie—mother of seven vaginally born children   96
    Thomas Ednie, M.D.—psychiatrist   100
    Rosemary Hayes—caesarean born artist   105
    Bruce King & Marilee James King—vaginally born/
        caesarean born couple   112
    Dennis McCracken—caesarean born social worker   117
    Jody Longnecker—caesarean born   118
    Sandy Hastings—potential caesarean mother   120
    Gayle Carlton—caesarean born rebirther   125
    Anne Stine—caesarean born therapist   131

Part IV—The Journey in Perspective
        and the Path Ahead   135

Annotated Bibliography   140

With appreciation
to all who helped along the way

Foreword

by Stanislav Grof, M.D., Ph.D.

How one is born seems to be closely related to one's general attitude toward life, the ratio of optimism to pessimism, how one relates to other people, and one's ability to confront challenges and conduct projects.

It is astounding that the nature and duration of birth has been ignored almost entirely by Western psychologists and psychiatrists. When birth was studied at all, the studies were more concerned about possible perinatal brain damage than the emotional significance of birth. Until quite recently, only a few studies explored the psychological significance of birth and of caesarean section, in particular.

This is especially alarming in view of the fact that since the advent of fetal monitoring which detects the slightest signs of fetal distress and because of increasing fear of malpractice suits, the rate of caesarean birth in some hospitals has skyrocketed to 40 percent. It is imperative that we learn about the psychological and social implications of such a drastic change in childbirth patterns.

Particularly relevant are the differences among individuals born by non-labor caesarean section, uncomplicated vaginal delivery, difficult vaginal birth, and emergency caesarean section. How do they differ in their basic personality, incidence of various emotional and psychosomatic disorders, life attitudes and strategies, interpersonal relationships, and political, philosophical and religious beliefs?

Jane English's research on being born non-labor caesarean represents a truly pioneering venture; she has sketched a much-needed first map of previously uncharted territories. She is particularly well-equipped to accomplish this difficult task. Being caesarean born, she has the necessary sensitivity, deep personal interest and motivations. Having had rigorous training in physics, she is well acquainted with the principles of scientific investigation and thinking. On the other hand, her personal experiences and interest in the new paradigms in science give her the freedom to explore new areas without the strait-jacket of traditional concepts of mechanistic science. Many of her conclusions based on experiential impression can provide inspiration for future controlled studies. This book may provide an incentive for future explorers and researchers to map systematically this important territory of the psyche.

One's overall life strategy can be deeply influenced by psychological work that includes the perinatal level of the unconscious. Under proper circumstances, reliving biological birth and integrating the experience into one's way of being seems to offer possibilities of psychosomatic healing, personality transformation and consciousness evolution that by far exceed therapy limited to work with biographical material from childhood and later life.

Since I was a facilitator in an important stage of Jane's personal quest, I particularly appreciate the value of her book for therapists. I learned important lessons from our often frustrating efforts to apply to her process the experiences and principles derived from work with vaginally born people. It is a tribute to her introspective ability and intelligence that she was able to identify the specifics of the caesarean personality in her own process, validate them by independent observations and formulate them in a way that will help others to avoid the pitfalls with which we struggled.

In a process that is by its nature pre-verbal and reveals itself through experiences which are hard to describe in words, any alternative mode of communication is of great value. The author's ability to express her personal journey through pictorial art adds an important dimension to her work.

Although *Different Doorway* will be of primary interest to caesareans, its significance is much more basic. Exploring the profound programming imposed on us by our early history is of great interest to all those interested in serious self-exploration, therapy, and philosophical and spiritual quests.

Experiential confrontation with birth and death function as a gateway to a vast domain of the human psyche that can be best described as transpersonal. It includes ancestral, collective and past incarnation memories; archetypal visions and entire mythological sequences; authentic identification with animals and plants; and extrasensory perception. We can no longer ignore the fact that the spiritual or transpersonal dimension is an inherent property of the human psyche.

Experiential work on prenatal and perinatal issues seems to lead to a new type of human being. Such a person has the capacity to appreciate and enjoy existence and shows deep spiritual feelings about the world. He or she has reverence for life, tolerance toward others, and understanding of interdependence in nature and society. This has far-reaching implications for the current global crisis and suggests alternatives to current strategies.

Stanislav Grof, M.D., Ph.D., is a psychiatrist who for thirty years has researched non-ordinary states of consciousness. He was born in Czechoslovakia where he received his scientific training. One of the founders of transpersonal psychology, he is currently Scholar-in-Residence at Esalen Institute, Big Sur, California. He is author of six books and over seventy articles in professional journals (see Bibliography).

Prologue

My interest in caesarean birth began in 1973. Ten years later in 1983, I finally had the opportunity to see a caesarean delivery.

My own birth was non-labor caesarean, and pictures and images of caesarean births had evoked strong reactions in me. I wondered what it was going to be like to actually see a caesarean birth. An obstetrician friend of mine who is herself caesarean-born invited me to watch her doing a caesarean. I had never seen surgery, but having been present at two home births, I had some experience of what it feels like to witness a child being born. The incredible opening to the infinite. The sense of something extraordinary happening. The sound of the first cry. The welcoming of a new being to the earth. I had experienced that, but I wondered how I would respond to seeing a body cut open, blood flowing and the organs revealed.

Much to my delight, I discovered that I was very clear. The inner work I had done on releasing the fear of cutting and blood stood me well.

The mother was given general anesthesia; a spinal hadn't worked. It was too bad the mother wasn't awake, but it was good for me to have this caesarean be like my own birth with general anesthesia.

I meditated while I watched. I paid attention to my thoughts, my feelings, my intuitions and my body. I tried to be aware of the quality of the consciousness in the room. It was emotionally intense. Underlying the professional competence was fear or anxiety. Afterward, the intern told me he always gets sweaty whenever he assists at a caesarean. That is his way of reacting to the intensity. It takes a lot of work to suppress such strong feelings. It's important for him to focus on the procedure, not on his feelings. But I wonder if medical people might be trained in the psychological and spiritual aspects of birth in order to come to terms with their gut responses to the cutting, the pulling out of the baby and the emotion.

I stood by the mother's feet and watched the knife and the surgical scissors cutting into the belly. There was not a twitch or quiver in my body. There was simply a feeling of "Yes, this is how it is done." The layers of flesh were shiny and beautiful, even the layers of fat. It was extraordinary to see the inside of a human body. All the pictures I had seen hadn't prepared me for the awesomeness of the experience.

Through all the cutting and suctioning, I admired the skill of my friend and the clarity of her communications with the intern, the anesthesiologist and the scrub nurse. When she cut through the abdominal wall and the uterus, I could see something dark. It was the baby's hair showing through the amniotic sac. It looked like another organ inside the woman's body. With retractors pulling the flesh back, my friend stuck her hand in just above the woman's pubic bone. She reached in behind this dark roundish thing, got one of her hands underneath and lifted.

A face appeared! That was the most awesome moment. This little human face rising up out of all the cut flesh and the blood. A human being entering the world through this different doorway, this extraordinary way to enter the world! And it *was* a birth. The same feeling of awe, of wonder, of sacredness I had felt at the home births. Yes, this is one more of us coming here to earth for whatever he or she has to experience and learn. In writing about it, I still find myself moved. I still feel the mystery and the wonder.

As I watched, I felt acceptance. It is OK to come in this way: the blood, the cutting, the abrupt intrusion, the emotions of the people, the awkwardness of it. Somewhere inside, I came to a deeper acceptance of how I was born. A big hand came down in and lifted me up, through all the blood, into a bright light.

The baby's first contact with another human being is that hand reaching in. Then the doctor suctions the baby's nose and mouth. I realized that as a child at the dentist's office, I had been re-experiencing the fear that had accompanied the sensations of the suction at my birth.

After the suctioning was complete, the doctor took hold again of the baby's head and pulled, delivering the rest of the body. I tensed up. The pulling was more than I could fully handle. I think the hardest part of my own birth was when they pulled on my head. It is like being killed. This little body that has been curled up is abruptly stretched, without the gradual stimulation of labor. There isn't just physical pain; there is an abrupt surge of energy through an organism which is not only totally unprepared but also drugged by the anesthesia. The body reacts in terror with shuddering and fear.

The baby girl's skin was bluish. One of the pediatricians held her above her mother and cut the umbilical cord before the baby started to breathe. Then the two pediatricians took her to the other side of the room to a warm padded table. They wiped her off, did more suctioning and vigorously stimulated her body to get breathing going. They also gave her some oxygen.

As I watched them rubbing the baby with towels, a little bit here and a little bit there, I remembered my own experience of feeling fragmented. Coming down the birth canal, the whole body is stimulated at once. This must give a sense of wholeness, of coherence, of integrity of the body.

Of course, all babies come out, are suctioned, wiped off and so forth, but those born vaginally have already gone through an important learning experience, an experience of their body. The suctioning or the wiping is not the first strong contact they experience. For a non-labor caesarean, the wiping is the labor. The wiping gives an intense experience of contact, of boundaries. The labor is not done by the mother; it is done by doctors and nurses. They might do it differently if they knew they were "laboring" with the child, were actually giving birth to the child.

It was perfect for me that the baby was a girl because I could identify more closely with her. I noticed that her genitals were engorged. That affirmed my own experience of the huge sexual arousal that is involved in birth. A lot of energy is moving through the body, and as it moves through the pelvic area it produces sensations that one later on learns to call sexual. In Stan Grof's work on vaginal birth, he talks about the high level of sexual arousal in the last part of labor, when the child is moving down the birth canal. Perhaps sexual arousal is universally part of birth, and for the non-labor caesarean it happen through the stimulation by the medical people. Birth is one's first sexual encounter. Seeing what was happening in that baby's body was an affirmation of my way of conceptualizing my experience. I said to myself, "I've been there. I know what it is like."

I stayed with the baby as long as she was in the operating room. Then I watched as the medical team tied the mother's tubes as she had requested. The uterus was lifted out of the abdominal cavity. It was amazing to see the ovaries and the fallopian tubes, these amazing structures within the body of every woman, the place from which our bodies come into this world.

Afterward the obstetrician took me to the nursery. A nurse was feeding the baby some sugar water from a bottle. The baby was sucking sluggishly. I imagined her feeling, "OK, so here I am. Now what?" She seemed not too excited and not particularly uncomfortable.

I thought of all those people who had handled this baby, giving her what she needed on the physical level. But it seemed the emotional and spiritual levels were not being nurtured. I hope this book is a step toward that. I hope there will be increasing respect for the fact that a caesarean operation is the birth of a human being.

We have taken steps toward doing caesarean birth technically well, and we have a lot more to learn. I think we have a wonderful adventure ahead of us.

Part I

The Territory

My words are the footprints of what I experience. No more and no less. They are not "just words," and they are not my experience. I can use them to express or to oppress myself. Anyone, including myself, who takes the words to be the reality of my experience will be confused and disappointed by the emptiness of the words.

Yet words are useful as signposts. As I experience new things, I sometimes remember reading what other people have written. This helps me accept my own experience, helps me be more open to it. Perhaps my writings similarly will help others.

—Journal, November 1, 1974

"Caesarean-born" as a Conceptual Tool

Part of every human experience has been the journey down the birth canal. Only during the last hundred years have there been many of us who didn't experience that, who were born caesarean. Although the medical procedure of caesarean delivery has become routine, we are just beginning to learn about the psychological and spiritual aspects of this different kind of birth. In this book I focus on the experience of the child in the caesarean delivery, rather than that of the mother.[1]

There are two kinds of caesarean deliveries: those done before labor starts and those done, often in emergency conditions, after some labor. I call these non-labor caesareans and labor caesareans, respectively. The usual medical terms, elective caesarean and non-elective caesarean, focus on the doctor's and mother's experience rather than on the child's. I am concentrating mainly on non-labor caesarean birth because I was born that way.

Thoughts and images of caesarean birth are for me a conceptual framework, a tool. My interest in using the concept "caesarean born" was not purely academic. It was motivated by great chaos and discomfort in my personal life. The thought of being caesarean seemed to bring some clarity and direction into what otherwise seemed a hopeless morass of emotion and failed relationships in my life. It also connected my body and feeling to the "light" I was pursuing in my photographic work.

This is a book of anecdotal material, not of scientific facts. I am not telling you what it is like to be born non-labor caesarean; instead I am sharing some of what I experienced during ten years of using "caesarean born" as an important part of my self-concept. While the material in this book is relevant to medicine, psychology, religion and other fields, I have chosen to stand outside of those frameworks and simply share this as a record of a journey.

I am, perhaps, beginning to create a map of the territory, pointing out some of the demons and some of the helpers I met on my path. I was inspired by Stanislav Grof's work.[2] I saw the wonderful map he made of vaginal birth and realized it did not fit my journey. I had to make my own map. But I learned from him that this kind of map is possible. Being born non-labor caesarean, my map is of that experience. People who were born in a caesarean delivery after some labor can take pieces of my map and of Stan's map and weave them together to fit their own experience. I was also inspired by Christina Grof's work with kundalini, taking her own intense inner journey and being able to share it objectively with other people.

I felt ambivalent about creating a map of caesarean birth. A conceptual framework can be a prison. People could use such a map to categorize

[1]Several good books have been written recently on the mother's experience of a caesarean delivery. See the bibliography.

[2]See Foreword and Bibliography

people, to not see them as they are. On the other hand, concepts can be liberating stepping-stones on one's path. I hope that caesarean-born people who have had experiences similar to mine will be able to use that similarity to affirm their own experiences. Perhaps they won't have to spend as much time and energy as I have denying and suppressing their experiences, both positive and negative.

Using caesarean birth as my conceptual framework is a temporary stage. It helps me make the transition from being unconsciously identified with birth patterns, past the temptation to use being caesarean as a justification for staying stuck in these patterns, and on to transcending them and moving into a greatly expanded awareness of what it is to be human.

Inner Exploration

This book is an adventure story, a story about explorers and exploration. I like to think of it being, in a small way, parallel to stories about exploration of the New World or of outer space. But there is a difference. For me, the unexplored territory was not a new continent or the farther reaches of the solar system. It was within my own being, in consciousness. It was my thoughts, my emotions, my perceptions and images and my physical form. The new frontier, as many others have noted, is inner space. Many oriental and so-called primitive cultures have detailed and complex technologies of body, mind and spirit. But we in the West, until recently, have been strangely lacking in this area. Several centuries of intensive exploration of the external world have led most people in the Western world away from the vast territory within themselves. Awareness of the inner territory is often suppressed by calling it crazy, unscientific or too subjective.

In the past century, psychiatry has attempted to remedy this lack, but much of the interpretation orthodox psychiatry gives to inner experience is that of pathology. Inner states are recognized only when they are bizarre and cause enough dis-ease to be labeled as diseases. Then the medical model is applied with its symptoms, diagnoses and treatments.

It is no wonder most of us learned at an early age not to talk about inner experience. To do so was to run the risk of being called crazy or sick.

I often use a story as a metaphor for my transition from outer explorations to inner ones. My exploring as a child and through my twenties was externally focused; bushwhacking through the woods and exploring the world of sub-atomic particle physics fascinated me equally. After completing my physics Ph.D., I worked for a short while in a research group at a particle accelerator. One day as I was looking into an oscilloscope (like a small TV screen) adjusting some electronic signals, I realized I was more fascinated with the reflection of my own eyes than I was with the signals. Those big eyes looking at me out of the greenish darkness. I thought I was going crazy. And in a sense I was. I was beginning to look into the inner territory I had grown up calling "crazy." A few years later my clear decision to do what I called "going crazy" without getting caught or labeled crazy was an essential step in starting the inner explorations that led to this book.

Recently it has become less necessary to carry the negative self-judgments associated with "crazy" in order to experience the territory hidden behind that label. Many individuals and groups have taken great steps in the past few decades toward legitimizing inner exploration in the context of our western scientific culture, and I am grateful to many of them for making my journey easier.

Reality

It became increasingly apparent to me that a much expanded view of reality is necessary when one is considering the phenomenon of birth. Birth is one of the boundaries of individual physical existence. To consider it only from the perspective of personality, of ego, of being a separate individual who has already been born, creates much distortion. It is as if one were to look at the walls of a house only from the inside and assert that the knowledge gained thereby is complete. We talk about a "person" being born. But when we use the word "person," we bring along with it our own unconscious assumptions of what it is to be a person. Many of these assumptions are based on our own experience of birth, the process in which our person is given a separate physical form. It is important that we be aware of these assumptions when we are with a person born in a way different from our own birth; we may not be seeing them clearly.

During my inner journey I had to greatly expand my idea of what is real, of what experiences are possible. I found myself believing in the ability to recall birth, in past incarnation memories and in spirit—ideas which previously seemed absurd to me.

Concepts of a transpersonal or spiritual reality served not only as explanations of my experiences, but also as tools for transformation. I came to see that many of my "problems" were the result of the physical and emotional tensions created in trying to stuff my experience, my humanness, into too small a conceptual framework. Concepts of expanded reality were stepping-stones or scaffolding that helped me accept what I was experiencing without judging it wrong or crazy, thus enabling me to release the tension.

My scientific training was both a help and a hindrance. On the negative side was my deeply entrenched belief in a logical, cause/effect, separative, Newtonian physics world. Judgments and denial coming from that part of myself very much slowed down my acceptance of experiences I had in transpersonal, spiritual or higher realms of consciousness.

On the other hand, the spirit of open exploration and inquiry I had cultivated as a physicist was helpful. Perhaps even more important was my experience of the amazing world of sub-atomic particle physics where reality indeed seems strange and paradoxical to anyone whose beliefs are based on the world of Newtonian physics. It prepared me for my adventures in the even stranger and more paradoxical world of consciousness.

Concepts of a larger reality helped me understand how my dream and inner experiences of people were related to my everyday experience of them. I wondered, "What is real, the person out there, my dreams of them, my thoughts of them or what?" Along the way various concepts, such as psychological projection, were at first helpful in clarifying the situation, though later they themselves sometimes became obstacles to further expansion and clarification.

In Part II of this book I have chosen to mention some people by name as they appeared in dreams, inner work or external encounters. I let them be evolving characters in the story. Each is partially my creation, partially a real human being and partially something from a realm of oneness where such distinctions are meaningless.

It is difficult to use words to describe the vast transpersonal or spiritual realms that are beyond and within this realm of separate physical existence. This is because words are themselves part of the limited physical world. The best we can do is to continually remind ourselves of the greater reality and to be aware of experiencing our limited existence in relation to it.

The Story

Part II of this book is a journal of my birth-related experiences and ideas from 1973 to 1983. It is not neat and logical. Material often emerged in a confusing, random way. I have had to resist a temptation to create a "story line" for the reader to follow.

In presenting lecture/slide-shows on this material I have often helped people understand the apparently random order of my experiences with a little demonstration. I crumple a sheet of paper into a ball. Then I draw a line on the surface of the ball. When I unfold the paper, the "line" appears to be a random series of markings, even though it was a relatively straight line on the crumpled ball. In just such a way at each moment of my journey I did what *felt* like moving straight ahead. It is only in retrospect, when the convolutions and crumples of my psyche are laid out in a linear, chronological way, as in this book, that the journey looks random and chaotic.

The process was one of peeling away veils of illusion, continually going deeper. Becoming aware of thoughts, emotions, images and physical tensions and actions. Seeing as optional what had always seemed real and absolute. Clearing away obstructions to full awareness of the miracle of being human.

New understandings didn't arrive full-blown and integrated into my ordinary waking consciousness. They appeared piecemeal, sometimes as partial truths. I have chosen to leave in the book many of the partial truths. They were stepping stones that supported me until I moved beyond them.

Early in the journey, much of my experience was jagged, raw and constricted, with only a few glimmers of light and clarity. Later on there was more balance, more awareness, more expansion and light. Darkness and constriction still overwhelm me occasionally, just as intensely as before. But this state usually doesn't last as long or come as often as before. Someone once said to me that being more enlightened doesn't mean one never experiences difficult passages, but one gains the awareness and the tools to move through them faster.

While I followed various practices with names such as gestalt, mindfulness meditation, rebirthing, sensory awareness, and light-fire meditation, I found as I progressed that the essential element of all of these was a non-judgmental witnessing, a simple awareness of thoughts, emotions, images and sensations. When I encountered a "problem" or a stuck, habitual pattern, non-judgmental awareness was in itself enough to bring release. The nature of being alive is to be changing.

Throughout the journal writings in Part II I use terms like "inner exploration," "inner work," "following process," and "awareness work" to describe the state of being with myself with the intention simply to be aware of my experience.

The outward manifestation varied. Sometimes I would sit or lie down with my eyes closed, although they might remain open. Or I would move about and allow emotional expression and sounds. Sometimes I was with a facilitator and sometimes alone.

In Part II, I let the journey unfold rather than giving explanations of everything as it happened. I want to let you, the reader, share in the adventure and to come to your own ideas about what was happening. Some of your ideas will be different from mine; neither are the absolute truth.

As you read each of the journal entries, you will enter into the unknown, not knowing where you are being led, just as I did. I have included descriptions of the process as well as the final insights for two reasons. First, I want to share what I have learned about the process of inner exploration. Second, words are at best a rough translation of the knowledge I am communicating. Emotions, images and bodily sensations often are closer to the source.

In using words, I am attempting to express myself in an unfamiliar dialect. The words are rooted in the body-language of vaginal birth. I am trying to communicate the body-language of non-labor caesarean birth. That is why I describe in such detail the physical experiences I had.

As I did inner non-verbal explorations, something would emerge into my awareness, and I would translate it into words. But the words are not the essence. They are mental, the element air. Birth is about coming into a body, about earth. The words are like feathers. Feathers are wonderful, but they have to be attached to a body before they can fly.

I ask you to read my words not just with your mind but with your body. You may have to read more slowly than usual and to be willing to feel what is happening in your body. You may run into your own conditioning, your own birth learning, things you have tried to suppress.

The inner journey began with my feeling alone, strange and different. As I continued on, I began to discover fellow travellers. The conversations in Part III are from the stage of my journey where I surface from the inner depths and began to share adventure stories with these fellow travellers, some of whom are caesarean born and some not.

Part II

The Journey

The process of getting totally entangled in illusion and then finding a way out is perhaps the ultimate adventure.

In the titles of most of the chapters of this section I mention one of the four elements: Earth, Air, Fire and Water. In traditions ranging from Ancient Greek to Native American, these four elements are used as symbols of four aspects of human consciousness. Air is the mental, conceptual level. Water is the emotional, fluid aspect of our being. Fire is the spiritual, the divine spark. It is also the intuitive, the flash of insight. And Earth is, of course, the physical, the body.

As I organized the material for Part II, I saw that in different periods of my inner journey, though all four were always present, one of the elements was predominant.

Chapter 1

Fire: Initiation

Except for reading a little about primal therapy, I had, prior to the following dream, little or no sense that one could recall the experience of being born. The dream was an initiation. It gave me an intuitive understanding of the new territory I was entering and sketched the path through it. It was a spark, the element fire, a gift from spirit.

At the time of the dream, I was living with people who shared dreams each morning, and I blithely shared this one. At that point, it was just words and images. I was not at all in touch with the emotions or the physical tensions involved. Awareness of these began about a year later and started me on the journey that is chronicled in the rest of this section.

The dream was truly a map. At times when I was deeply immersed in negativity, I would remember the dream and know there was a way out.

The Dream—sometime in 1973

I am lying drugged and unable to move on my back on a high table in the right front room of a big old house. My mother lies on top of me and rapes me. Even in the dream I am aware of the impossibility of being raped by a woman. Lots of sexual feelings and a sense of total defeat, of being overwhelmed physically and psychologically. I withdraw deep into myself and give up.

Then I feel resentment. I see her standing by a wall to my right. I go over to her and tear her belly open with my hands. Great rage as I kill her.

Then I walk out into the front hall. It is an empty room with several closed doors.

I open the one to the left front room and find it full of strangers. I feel alone and uneasy.

I sit by one of the front windows. One by one the people bring me gifts. I realize this is my birthday party. I feel happy.

The extreme violence in the dream is symbolic of the physical and emotional intensity of birth. It does not reflect my current feelings toward my mother. I also should include here the facts of my birth as told me by my mother. I was born non-labor caesarean because my older brother was caesarean. It was done a week ahead of time because the doctor had scheduled his wedding for my due date. My mother was given ether as a general anesthesia. I was brought to her 24 hours later. She tells me I was "tight-lipped." "If a baby could say NO, you were doing it." I refused to breast feed. Finally, 48 hours after birth, bottle feeding was begun.

The dream expresses in symbolic language my memory of birth. The drugging is the anesthesia. The rape is the violation and intrusion I felt when the doctor cut my mother open. I was biologically and psychically unified with her, so I also experienced the invasion. This happened in the context of my mother's body, my whole world up to that time, so it seemed that she, not the doctor, was invading me. The murderous rage is related to anger I felt as the doctor and his assistants roughly stimulated me to get breathing started. This happened just outside my bloody cut-open, apparently dead mother,[3] so I seemed to be angry with her, not the doctor. The empty hall is related to being alone in the nursery. The strangers were all the people who handled me that first day. Later I experienced them as nourishers bringing me gifts at my birthday party.

The pioneering work of Stanislav Grof has showed me the importance and the possibility of transforming the roots of violence that lie subconsciously within all of us. These are often associated with suppressed memories of birth, either vaginal or caesarean. In his work, survivors of concentration camps found that memories of the physical and psychological agonies they experienced in the camps were less intense than memories of what they had experienced in birth. According to Grof, the intensity of the pressure, pain, fear, suffocation, helplessness and rage, and the physical pleasure, excitement and ecstasy experienced in vaginal birth is the most intense thing a human ever experiences.

It is my intention to show that a caesarean birth is not less or more intense. It is simply different.

In Greek mythology, Dionysius (Bacchus) is the god of revelry and also of madness. His challenge to humans is, "If you won't dance the lesser dance of madness (symbolic acting out of intense emotion in revelry and bacchanalia), I will force you to dance the greater dance of madness (psychosis, violence)."

My dream was an invitation and a warning to dance the lesser dance. I was fortunate that about a year afterward I was in therapeutic situations where I could begin to safely release the emotions, images and physical tensions the dream symbolizes. It is likely that if I had tried to suppress the dream, my life would not have moved in the positive direction it has over the past few years.

July 22, 1974   Journal

I see how I control myself. Always alert, on top of things, not giving in to the flow. Two years ago a friend called me "control mad." He was right. Now I think I understand that it comes from never having been born properly. I think of my anesthetized caesarean birth. Peace in the womb, fading into the drug, waking up in a harsh world. No connected transition. No wonder I resist letting go. I had an awful experience that first time. So now I am beginning to let myself be born, to go with the flow.

[3]Other people whose mothers were anesthetized at birth have spoken of the feeling of having killed their mother. See the interview with Gayle Carlton in Part III.

Chapter 2
Water: Inner Depths

During 1974 there were major changes in my life. Intense discomfort and dissatisfaction motivated me to begin deep inner exploration of emotions, dreams, body and thoughts. Initial steps were a five-day workshop at Esalen Institute[4] in Big Sur, California, and reading books on experiential psychology and inner exploration. In the fall I moved to Esalen and ended my relationship with Gia-fu Feng, with whom I did a translation of Tao Te Ching. *That book was important in my life, both because of its content and because of the financial support it brought me. Only half jokingly I tell friends that the explorations that led to this caesarean book were funded by Lao Tsu.*

Looking back on my time at Esalen, I see I was exploring the repressed, forbidden parts of myself. I decided to "let what may" surface into awareness. I remember thinking I wanted to "go crazy" without getting caught. It was an exciting, scary and not particularly comfortable time as I dove into the emotional, water element of my being. During this time the fire element continued in the form of vivid dreams and flashes of insight.

Of all the workshop leaders, the one I trusted and respected most was Dick Price, one of the founders of Esalen. He seemed equally at home with intense emotional and physical expression and with subtle, meditative states of being. In a quiet, compassionate, no-nonsense way he led people deep into the core of their being. I did the following work with him during a month-long workshop. At the time I didn't consciously connect it with birth, though in retrospect it seems to be about the obstetrician pulling on my head to bring my body out.

November 27, 1974   Work in Dick Price's workshop

We did an exercise in which we picked a word. I said, "sad." Then we associated it to a body part—"chest" for me. Then picking another word, "moving," I associated this with my head. Then I decided to explore this with Dick. I started with my head saying, "I'm moving on to new and exciting things. I am really free now. A lot of things are happening. I'm opening up. This is great." Body replied, "You've gone on too fast and left me behind. I'm sad and lonely." Then I felt empty. Dick told me to explore the emptiness, but I refused and began to push it away. I pushed out on Dick's arm as he gently pushed into my chest with his other hand. "I won't." Then more withdrawing from his push. "I won't let you touch me.

[4]The Bibliography can be used as a resource directory, giving access to the various tools and techniques I used in the journey.

I'll stop feeling." But I felt pain I couldn't block out. Dick asked who I was talking to. I didn't know. I kept repeating, "I won't let you touch me." Terror, tight body, lots of tension. Through this, I was thinking, "This is just a game. I am playing the same games I always do." Then I realized that labeling my experience as a game is an avoidance of the experience. A way of not accepting what I do as being real.

I stopped calling it a game and relaxed into "there is nothing I have to do." Then, Dick helped me pay attention to emptying and filling with breath. I breathed in and out, feeling myself let go. Opening up, especially high in my chest. When I breathed into that area, I felt ecstasy rising in me. Close to wanting to cry for myself, compassion for me. Relaxing my whole body. I said, "There's a new space up here at the top." Dick asked, "How does that space feel?" I said, "Peaceful, happy." More breathing. This all felt like a deep meditation. Then he asked me to allow my awareness to move back and forth from head to body. I found head saying a simple "hello" to body. Later I felt very connected and good. Feeling love and caring from myself and from Dick.

Another of the first people who guided me in the inner wilderness I had entered was Paul Rebillot. He said I was embarking on a journey and suggested I keep a journal. Inspired both by his own experience of a journey through madness and by Joseph Campbell's book Hero With a Thousand Faces, *Paul began to conduct workshops at Esalen entitled "The Hero's Journey." Each participant became aware of his or her own inner hero and inner demon. I was astounded when the following material emerged spontaneously and vividly. It was the first time birth material had come to me while awake.*

December 1, 1974   Hero's Supreme Ordeal fantasy
On coming up over the grassy hill to a "360-degree view of my worst fear," I see myself lying on a table with either my guts or an umbilical cord hanging off me, a gray organic tube lying on the stomach. The head is to the left, feet to the right as I approach the body from the side. No clear sense of the surroundings except that there is a lot of light. I wonder, "Is this my birth scene?" The face is bloody, mouth open as if screaming, eyes wide open, a look of terror. I surface from the fantasy. Paul tells me to confront it. I spend a long time alternately looking and avoiding.

Then a feeling of "I've got to eat it." I put my mouth around the gray tube. My face seems to be in the blood on the stomach. I relax and breathe, opening my mouth and allowing it to feel filled. I think about breast feeding attempted by my mother and wonder if there is a connection.

Then I remember the "secret weapon" I had chosen as part of the workshop. I had chosen "The Void." I spend a while exploring how to use it. I decide "If I am empty inside and the emptiness is the infinite Void, then it is OK to let this (the guts I have to eat) come in." More relaxing.

I couldn't or wouldn't complete the fantasy. I started to discount the whole thing. But the fantasy was something that did arise in my inner space and slowly will lead me through whatever I need.

December 4, 1974

Watching a friend's exploration facilitated by her daughter, I felt how painful my connections with women are. I envied my friend's clear, open relationship—such a different mother/daughter relationship from me and my mother. So I asked for help in exploring "women." I told each woman in the group how I push her away. Then I remembered that awful dream of rape, murder and birthday party. I hesitated, then let myself experience it more fully. I acted out some of the rage. Then I felt overwhelmed, gave up and cried. I curled into fetal position and slowly worked out of it, experiencing my body as being weird pinks and purples, bony and stringy. This was after 32 hours of fasting. I decided to eat soon, pleased the fast had led me deeper into myself. The next morning I felt softer and more feminine.

January 15, 1975

In the morning I had deep tissue massage work. An image arose as she worked deep in my belly. Me, as a child, standing in the bathroom upstairs in my childhood home and Mother getting out of the shower. I see the scar across her stomach. She tells me that was where she was cut open when I was born. Another image arose of me standing in the kitchen, punching her in the belly. I was small. Eyes at the level of her waist.

In the afternoon I explored this, facilitated by Dick. I was feeling good: the body work had relaxed me. I went into the first image and found myself saying, "I'm sorry, I didn't want to hurt you," to Mother. Then I switched roles and became Mother facing Jane and said, "This is where they cut me open to take you out." Switched back to being me, feeling horror and disgust rippling through my body. Pulling in all over, shaking. "I don't want to look at your body." Seeing the scars, seeing her face squinched up, knowing that my face squinches up in the same way, feeling tension, pushing her away with my hands, then a strong feeling of not wanting to touch her. Hands and arms shaking wildly between push and withdraw. Pushing on Dick's arm, really feeling with my hands. Horror, revulsion—feeling flesh, quivery—amazing dance between his body and hands and my hands. All through this were clear images of Mother. This is new to have the images and feelings together. Finally I shut off and stopped feeling. Mouth clamped shut. "I'd rather die than let you in." This evoked waves of connections for me. There must be something even farther back behind this. Then slowly softening with breathing, I came back once more to touching with feeling—hands palm to palm with Dick's.

Figure 1—Pink Teddy

Later in the afternoon we did a group exercise on dream images. I came to Pink Teddy (a childhood teddy-bear) in the dream of the previous night. Image of the zipper in the belly of the teddy. (*See Figure 1*) Someone asked, "Do babies come out of it?" I first rejected this idea; then I suddenly made the connection between the zipper and Mother's scars. I got a rush of heat throughout my body, warm hands, warm feelings for teddy transferred to Mother. Wanting to hug her. Still shivers of revulsion alternating with wanting to hold her. This is the doorway for more work to come. The feeling is of revulsion combined with longing.

January 16, 1975   Dream
  Countryside of rolling green hills. One area is fenced off. I am given a map that labels it "Keystone Park."

This dream pointed to the importance of the previous day's experience. It and the following dream seem to be guidance from a deeper or higher part of myself, the part that has perspective and knows the way. Such dreams seemed to come when I felt most lost, depressed or crazy in my waking state.

January 26, 1975   Dream
  I am going to an oak tree that a little girl wants to cut down. I tell her to cut only the dead parts. We walk down a muddy slope. At the bottom is a swamp. I look for a way to cross it; there is no way. I go upstream, looking for a way around. It is hard going. As I see the oak tree ahead, I also see a path leading to the left. I go up it into a small house with windows facing uphill toward the oak. I realize that the windows are in my way. I backtrack to the main trail and go on up through the woods to an open, grassy hilltop that has a view of the surrounding soft, wooded hills. I feel good. A man is here with me. To my left are lower hills, and to the right, meadows and a rocky mountaintop. Gray clouds, fog and rain are up there, also down among the hills to the left. It is sunny where I am. I think, "More storms to come, and right now I am OK."

February 3, 1975
  Last night I was aware of a vague feeling involving a near drowning when I was two or three. I thought of my longings for a man, of my emotional attachments to Paul and to Dick, of the faceless male companion in my dreams, and of the person to whom I continually explain myself in my inner dialogue. This morning I remembered the drowning. I sensed the filmy greenness of being underwater, allowing the feeling of drowning until the pain in my chest demanded I breathe again. There is a lot of feeling here. Twice I was yanked out of bliss—when I was born and when I was saved from drowning. I owe my life to a man; I blame my life on a man. The near-drowning was in some ways a re-run of my birth.

February 4, 1975
  I am at Esalen in the garden. The sun is shining brilliantly. Dick is there taking time to be with himself. The colors around him are bright, and he seems happy. Then he and I walk on a new path in the woods. The ground in covered with a beautiful green vine with purple flowers, no weeds. Beams of sunlight shine here and there through the trees. The new path is somewhat walked on, but not yet worn down to bare earth.

I later learned that Dick, like myself, was born caesarean.

*After about eight months at Esalen, I felt even more off balance. A lot
had been stirred up in me, but I hadn't released much of it in a lasting way.
I left Esalen and spent the summer of 1975 visiting friends and family in
Wisconsin, New Hampshire and California, and participating in a
Sensory Awareness workshop led by Charlotte Selver in Maine. During
these outer travels the inner journey continued.*

July 15, 1975

Paying attention to what I am feeling. Sense of a cold machine in me.
Then something to do with cutting warm, soft flesh and breaking a bubble.
Physical horror and shuddering. I wonder if at some level I was aware of
the whole caesarean operation.

July 23, 1975

Waking early with an image of me lying in a green forest. I explore a
sense of opening in my chest. Rolling onto belly and experiencing tension
in my front-side. Afraid of letting go. Curling up, then lying on my back,
afraid I'll fly apart. A sense of "me" returns when I hold my breath. Then
anger emerges. Pushing away. Images of people. "I don't want to live for
you." (Then a long list of people in my life.) This all deeply felt. Pushing
against the wall over my head. Breathing shaky and deep. Feeling a
scream wanting to come. I don't let it. Then a scary holding of breath.
Maybe reliving almost drowning. People above me trying to make me
breathe. Maybe part of the birth too. Strong sense of how I live and
especially how I breathe for someone else. Then, "I can breathe for myself.
I don't have to breathe to please you. I can do it to nourish myself." Crying,
then peace. This is such important work for me.

September 15, 1975

Feeling a lot of sexual energy. Fear. Image of knife cutting soft flesh.
Image of mother being cut open for me to be born. Babies happen because
of sex. Knives, babies, sex all mixed together.

September 18, 1975

I started exploring alone. Scared. Needing to be with someone. Went to
a friend. Felt comfortable with her. Withdrawing deep into myself. Then I
reach out from the bottom of a dark space. Panic, then regress, baby cry,
then opening, sucking, feeling warmth in my chest. Feeling nourished. She
held me, then gave me some tea.

*In the fall of 1975, I decided to participate in a nine-month Sensory
Awareness study group Charlotte Selver was teaching in California. I felt
the work would help me find more balance and quiet and also allow the
inner journey to continue. After travelling for a few months, the idea of
nine months of structured time appealed to me.*

November 11, 1975
Writing to help understand what I am experiencing

At some level I don't believe I am alive. All my so-called living has been negative. I live out of fear. I never chose to live. I exist in limbo, neither dead nor alive. Dying seems preferable. I've always done what people told me to do. I don't know why I am here. I'm not real. I'm a machine with no heart, ruthless. No wonder people are scared of me. I can't even die. This bleak hell is eternal. I'll go to sleep now. Maybe I'll be lucky and never wake up.

January 3, 1976   Exploration alone
Lying awake, I think of the rape/kill/birthday party dream from a few years ago. Image of mother as dead. I ask myself, "How do you know she is dead?" I reply, "She's leaning against the wall very still, and her stomach is open and bloody." I experience baby Jane seeing dead mother. "I killed you. I am evil." Switching roles to becoming mother. "I'm dead; my baby is gone. She's gone across the hall, and other people will take care of her." Then as mother, I say, "I want my baby back inside me. I'll eat my baby." Image of starting with foot. Waves of guilt. Imagining people are horrified. Chewing, almost vomiting, staying with it.

After a rest I let myself become baby Jane, only the body image is maybe that of a 3-year old. I go into the birthday party room and lie back on some pillows. I just stay there, not trying to make anything happen. Then, "There are people here, but I don't know anybody." It is a sunny, warm room. At first I don't like not knowing anyone. I feel scared.

They bring me gifts. I fully see the people for the first time and realize they are not threatening. A room full of strangers who want to help me. "Of course, I don't know them. I've just been born." Then I say to them, "You don't want anything from me; you just want me to live." Crying. Realizing I don't have to know someone to accept what they bring me. Images of Dick and Paul. Saying to them, "You didn't want anything from me; you just wanted me to live."

After writing all this, I reveled in joy and laughter, lying there in peace, feeling accepted. Letting in life, energy and love. Then awareness that I was alone. Noticing a tendency to discount this beautiful work because I was alone.

Later I thought of the image of "the thing I fear the most"—me lying on a table, stomach cut open, bloody, a gray tube running from my belly down my right leg. I had eaten the gray tube to absorb it back into me. This connects to mother-eating-child experienced today. Through a lot of this birth memory, I find myself experiencing Mother's role. Was I so much one with her that I felt it from her perspective as well as from mine? Being cut open, dying, separated from the baby. I'm glad I haven't had children yet. I couldn't have handled it, and this legacy of pain, death and blood would have been unconsciously handed on to another generation to live through.

I see that I get my nourishment from strangers. One of the strangers was the woman I met the day after my birth who always said she was my mother. I felt my mother had died at my birth. This woman was good to me, but she didn't seem to be Mother. As a child I used to scream at her, "You're not my mother." I think we have done all right in our relationship, considering that what surfaced today has been subconsciously within me.

In the earlier work with Paul, the baby-eating-cord is an expression of the desire for re-union with what had seemed to be part of me. (The cord is one's friend and companion for 9 months.) The mother-eating-baby is also an attempt to deal with separation. The boundaries between mother, child, cord and placenta are not well-defined. At the time of these experiences I was not aware of the work of other birth researchers that also speaks of such things.

January 23, 1976   After a sensory awareness class
In class we discussed working with images, feelings and memories that emerge during inner exploration. The idea is to re-experience them without exaggerating or repressing them. Then one can see that they are old patterns and that the present is new.

January 27, 1976
A few days ago I experienced a closing and tightening in my throat and chest. It seemed that "I" wasn't doing it. When I relaxed the knot simply got tighter. I stayed with it as long as I could.

Finally I sat up because I couldn't stand it. I felt shaken and naked. I imagined someone holding me with one hand on my chest and one between my shoulder blades. I lay on my right side, curled up and let my mouth go into sucking movements. Quite abruptly the sucking stopped. What was left was the familiar knot in my throat and chest.

What a connection. Sucking and choking simultaneously. The sucking had emerged alone in some explorations, but I'd never noticed it was accompanied by choking.

I cried a little with relief brought by the recognition. Then I slowly drank a glass of water. For the first time I allowed myself to fully experience the process of sucking and swallowing. I remembered the opening and warmth I felt when I worked with a friend in August.

A few days later, Natalie and I talked about my need to ask for attention in ways that are fulfilling to me. I told her I had discovered that I have been asking for nourishment and choking myself at the same time.

May 21, 1976
Hiking in the woods, I wandered off the trail looking for a safe place. Finally I found soft needles inside a circle of redwoods. I lay there for a long

time, then curled up and went deep inside to a quiet place. Soon I felt myself resisting some outgoing energy that was starting to happen. Then I allowed the movement and unfolded gently. "I was unfolded too soon." Later I found out a friend's baby was born by caesarean that day. She's afraid the baby will have to work through the birth later with some "pillow pounding." I'm not sure; one bad experience can be mitigated by later good ones, especially when the baby has a mother who is conscious of such things.

June 24, 1976

Feeling tense, being hard on myself. After intense mental and physical resistance came a cry for help. Then quiet. I let go of breathing. "I don't have to live; I don't have to breathe." After that, breathing was very erratic, but it was happening of itself. I wasn't forcing it. Afterward, I understood something. Last year when I said to Dick, "You have done exactly what I wanted you to do," I was as shocked as he was. I didn't know what I meant. Now I knew. He had been telling me to breathe! Both in birth and in the near-drowning a man helped me start breathing. So I have been going about manipulating, trying to get the help in breathing that I felt I needed, but couldn't ask for.

In July 1976, after almost two years of intense inner exploration, I moved to Mendocino, a small village 150 miles north of San Francisco as a place to rest. There I had friends from Esalen and from the sensory awareness work. So I felt it was a good place to create a bridge back into the world, without suppressing my inner journey. I first spent about five months mostly externally focused. Then in December, I attended a lecture/slide show in which Stan Grof presented his work on the psychological and spiritual aspects of vaginal birth. I was inspired by this to think more about the caesarean experience. It also stirred up the images, emotions and body tensions connected with my birth. I realized that the inner adventure was calling me again, so I plunged back in. I travelled several times to Esalen for workshops led by Stan and Christina Grof.

December 5, 1976   Inner exploring with a friend

Going way inside myself. Great fear. Crying, thrashing around and choking. Red color, blinding light. Feeling I am being killed. Obviously birth stuff. Holding onto my friend helped some.

December 26, 1976   Inner exploring with Stan and Christina

Emerging from a blank place to find Stan massaging my spine. Afraid that I'd stopped breathing and that he was trying to get me to breathe. Connecting this to the doctor starting my breathing at birth. Then experiencing an icy, numb, foggy feeling, and gray, red, blue electric colors. I became quieter and more numb, whole body feeling the way my jaw does when the dentist injects Novocaine. Then scary, intense gasping and thrashing. Seems connected with the anesthesia.

January 6, 1977   Inner exploring with Stan and Christina

On my stomach with Stan and Christina pushing on my head and shoulders. I push back and struggle and cry out. I really felt my existence in that. No longer disoriented or scared.

January 7, 1977

Natalie, who was with me in the sensory awareness group last year, did some sensing exploration with me. I lay on my back; she sat behind my head and moved it gently. I trusted her. At one point, she gently pushed my head into my neck. I experienced a fiery, burning sensation in my upper chest, throat, neck, and across the top of my shoulders. I was releasing some tension I had never released before. It seems associated with birth, with holding my head as they pulled me out. The sensations and emotions were strong. I got scared and stopped. It was more than I was ready to handle. But it was a beginning.

January 17, 1977

Tension in my face and neck. Then sensation at the top of my head. Pushing it against the wall, some of the same feeling as when working with Natalie. As I pushed, the ringing sound in my head stopped abruptly. I noticed the sudden quiet.

January 17, 1977

More work on the neediness I feel so much of the time. I think of the tension I begin to create with Stan. Then I understand it and cry in relief. I project onto whatever man is working with me all the desperate fear and hope I felt with the doctor at birth and with the man who rescued me from drowning. Sadness at the impasse I have come to with each man I have worked with as they take personally the desperation I project.

April 11, 1977   Work with Stan and Christina on my birthday

Going into a baby space. Internal movement and churning. Confusion, fear, feeling I am being re-organized and am turning into jelly, into organic ooze. Great holding in gut and in breathing. Not knowing what is happening to me, and feeling I've got to know or something terrible will happen to me. Great unfamiliarity with body. It seems like some awkward, fumbling thing I am trapped in. It doesn't seem to work right.

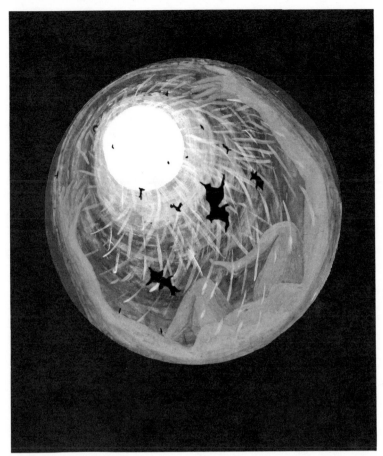

Figure 2—The Well

Images and sensations of falling backwards away from a bright light into a red hole, like a well. Dark forms are falling toward me. Intense fiery sensation in my body. (*See Figure 2*)

Later I feel totally reactive, no sense of "me." Am being created by the surroundings, feeling like a puppet. Images of a doctor's office, and of an Aztec Indian priest with a painted face.

April 27, 1977

Too soon, always too soon. Having to let go before I'm ready. Then wanting more and feeling wrong for wanting more. Even when I have enough, I am afraid my needs won't be filled the next time. So I hang on to what I've got.

Figure 3—The Ether Demon

May 14, 1977   Inner journeying while listening to music.

I go into a beautiful, open place and begin to see a big snowy mountain. Then I see a large, bear-like creature on its hind legs, walking toward me. Its fur is jagged; the colors are those I associate with the anesthesia at birth. Blue/white/red electric bear, icy cold mountain. A little fear. I cry some. Then he takes me into his arms. He turns from being a monster into being a protector and nourisher. Much love for this creature. No longer any sense of being alone. I feel safe, energized and happy. (*See Figure 3*)

May 16, 1977

Anger focusing on Mother's belly. Memory of punching her in the belly when I was four. Fantasy of chewing. Taste of blood. Memory of my surprise yesterday when I reacted to the line, "And you won't mind if I'm just a bit bloodthirsty," as I helped a friend rehearse his lines for "The Mikado." Now an overwhelming recognition of being bloodthirsty, literally. Mother's blood was my first taste. I feel intense sensations in my face and mouth. All the wanting, longing, hurt, anger and fear of death that surrounded birth are associated with the taste of Mother's blood. Memory of Christina's dream-image drawing of an adult female "baby" lying in a pool of blood. The "adult baby" in her drawing was right. As an adult I still have within me the bloodthirsty baby.

Yesterday was Mother's Day, and I resisted calling my mother. I was glad when the line was busy. With that bloodthirsty feeling so close to the surface, it is no wonder I resisted. Now I do want to call her.

May 20, 1977

I need to move, but against some resistance. It is a delicate dance, finding enough resistance so I can feel my own energy, yet gentle enough that I still feel safe and protected.

This is the process that feels like "being born" to me. Discovering myself in relation to external presence, creating boundaries, limits, a sense of "me." When I have a limit that feels right, I no longer have to constrict in order to protect myself. Nor do I have to create conflict between myself and others in order to feel some definition.

Perhaps the feelings of conflict and constriction are what is called ego, the false sense of "me." The unconflicted sense of "me" I get from "being born" feels different, more right, more free, more original and existing of itself.

June 19, 1977

I was asked about "residual tension" at the end of working with Stan. My reply was, "Well, there's the residual tension I call "being alive." I realize now that this is the place where the fear of dying begins. The fear seems to go deeper than anything personal with Stan, and for now he seems to trigger it in me. It seems like an opportunity, a door to open. . . .

Later: I think I held my breath just now without realizing it and slipped through the open door, so to speak. A being that is Stan/demon/monster bear/Aztec priest seemed to be attacking me. Terror, then explosion of breath and the sense that at my birth I was reliving a killing, perhaps from another incarnation. In this lifetime it was a birth, not a death. Now it is transformed. I lay on the bed shaking. Experiencing the bear on May 14th as being friendly gave me the courage to experience this today. My birth happened so fast. I think of Tom Ednie describing the frantic atmosphere surrounding both baby and mother in a caesarean birth. Trying to stop the mother's bleeding, trying to start the baby's breathing.

Body manifests as tensions and actions the unconscious memories I hold onto. Bringing them to consciousness releases them and allows them to de-materialize.

July 12, 1977

A friend spoke of grief as a natural process, the separation of two beings that have been one. It requires a readjustment on a cellular level. Crying is part of that. This immediately connected for me to birth, a separation I have never fully mourned. I wonder if the anesthesia prevented me from doing so. I think of the great raw place I feel in myself. It may have no psychological content and may be at this cellular level, the tearing apart of two beings. I have projected it onto the surgery, onto learning to breathe, onto people, onto the whole world. At its root, it is a psychic wound.

Figure 4a—The Pregnant Castle

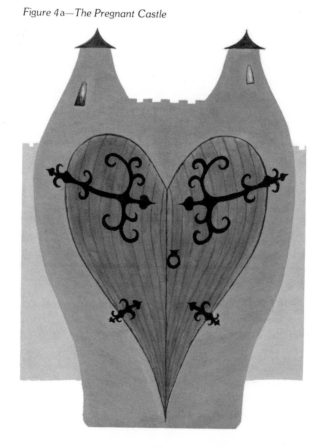

August 9, 1977

Sick for five days with flu, headache, tension, fever. A friend massaged my feet. I cried, and she held me and mothered me. Beautiful. Getting what I need. Then aware of how easily the need turns to anger at not having had enough. Good to be with a friend.

August 10, 1977

Waves of nausea that I somehow welcomed, knowing I have blocked that feeling a lot. Today I sketched the next painting in my series from a waking dream/vision. It is a castle (*See Figure 4*) breaking apart, opening, showing a baby. It fits with the nausea. Nausea is one of the side effects of ether, the anesthesia used at my birth. Usually I experience it as negative emotion or as a distaste for everything in the world. Such a revelation to experience it simply as nausea.

Figure 4b—The Castle Opening

Figure 5—Baseball Dream

August 11, 1977   Dream (*See Figure 5*)

Near second base on a baseball field. Talking with some friends, I take a step and my right foot goes through into a hole in the ground. It leads to a small tunnel. I see a wooden trap door leading to a side tunnel. I'm wary of the trap door, but a young man with curly hair goes in. I'm afraid for him. It is a tight squeeze. After a while he emerges looking like he's been through hell. He says there wasn't any air, just a sticky, sweet gas. He almost passed out, but he managed, with great effort, to crawl back out. I seem to be part way down the hole as I talk to him. I can see a room under the baseball field, maybe a locker room. It is a functional place with bluish-white lights. I ask if he will return to the surface with me, and he says he won't yet. He needs to digest what happened. He seems dazed.

Later, Christina and I agreed the dream has something to do with birth.

About three years later I understood this dream more fully. It is indeed a birth dream. It relates to the time when the head has been delivered and the body is still inside. Second base is halfway through the process. Head is out in the world seeing clearly; body is still inside, full of anesthesia and not ready to come up to the surface, not ready to be born. The locker room clearly is the operating room.

During September 1977, I participated in a workshop on "Maps of Consciousness," coordinated by Stan and Christina Grof at Esalen. A lot more material emerged for me. In the years since then, I have more and more appreciated having been in that workshop. Many seeds were planted there.

September 6, 1977   Music/breathing experience

Lying on the floor with the group, listening to music and following breath, I went through many emotions. Eventually I became very open and vulnerable. I thought that perhaps I have to become the rescuer, to dissolve boundaries and include the rescuer in my consciousness, in order to become whole. Then I let go of images of Stan watching the group, of him as protector and potential rescuer, and I was filled with white light.

During this time, I was frequently in intense states of confusion, resentment, frustration and depression. Yet I stayed with some deep inner knowing that understanding my caesarean birth was the way out, though there were moments I wanted to abandon the whole thing.

In the process of editing the writing I did during those years, I was again feeling angry, frustrated and stuck. Not knowing how to communicate and afraid of turning off readers. But then I saw my present feelings as yet another echo of what I had experienced earlier. I saw that the writing was OK just as it was, and that leaving difficulties out would imply that the process of transformation proceeded more easily and smoothly than it did. Being stuck was part of my process, perhaps a part I hadn't been willing to accept open-heartedly and without criticism. I began to experience compassion and understanding for who I was during those stuck years.

September 7, 1977   Unable to sleep, 2 a.m.

I want Stan to set limits for me so I won't die. Part of me wants to make him part of me. Then I'd be whole. My birth didn't happen naturally. I don't feel responsible for it. I need someone constantly to give birth to me. That is my dependence.

Wide awake now. Maybe I will stay up all night. Fantasy of having already fallen off the cliff, complete freedom. I'm dying, so anything goes. Connection between my birth and wanting to be killed, wanting the man who birthed me to finish the job by killing me. Then wanting to kill the rescuer/birther. All this assumes that the rescuer and I are separate beings. The way out seems to be through merging. We have to trust that if we surrender to a merger, we will then find ways to lead separate lives, each feeling whole. I wonder about the specifics of Stan's fear of being stuck with my dependence. I feel bad, wrong and crazy when I try to deny the intense attraction to a rescuer/healer. The desire to avoid feeling crazy is becoming stronger than the fear of rejection. Choosing to work with Stan is choosing to trust there is a way out of the present conflict.

Blah, blah, blah, blah, blah. I don't want to find a way out. I want to die. Why live? The only reason is to not upset people around me. As a child I used to play at hanging myself, but would stop for fear I'd botch it and be punished if Mother caught me. I tried to escape from life when I fell into the pond. Anger at the man who rescued me. I want to die, and I refuse to take responsibility for killing myself. What is my attachment to staying embodied? Fantasy of crawling into Stan's lap and dissolving while he and Christina dissolve, too. Dissolution is what all my violent fantasies are defenses against.

September 9, 1977

Last night was Stan's death/rebirth slide show. As in April, I felt sad, needy, fearful, and unable to get what I want. I want to work with Dick on this, but he isn't available. What a paradox. It seems the only way out will be to give up wanting to work on these deep feelings of wanting. I don't know how to do that.

A dream fragment from last night of being away from shore with wave after wave breaking over me, some picking me up high, then letting me fall a sickeningly long way. Fear, not knowing how to get out of this.

This connects with feeling bad and wrong. Nothing I do is right, in the sense that it gets me out of this situation.

So long as I attach the image of the source of nourishment to any one person, I am in a precarious place. That person can leave, die or forget me, and I end up wanting what isn't available. All my attempts to manipulate my environment, to get what I want only add to my insecurity and dependence.

I wonder if the experience of a perinatal no-exit situation is something necessary to human existence. Most people get it in the first part of labor; mine centers on hunger, need, etc. The dynamic is what Stan described last night. It is clear that the way out of the unsatisfied needing is to give up my sense of separateness. Each time I do this in a small way, the need begins to be filled. I begin to trust the wholeness of the universe. When I am willing to give up ego and to experience a feeling of connectedness. I feel no hunger. Instead a warm glow fills me.

September 10, 1977   Work with Stan and Christina

Shaking, high energy, rage just under the surface. "I don't want to fake it anymore." Willing to take risks. We talked about how to experience primal rage without hurting myself or others. A baby body can't be destructive in acting out the feelings; an adult can.

When we started to work, the rage was no longer on the surface. I went into chaos, fear and confusion. Image of white walls. Then chalky taste of milk of magnesia. Deeper into choking. I understood I had to go into the choking. Fear of dying, fear of killing myself by mistake. These verbalized, finally. Then it changed. I felt it as a contest, rather than as me being choked. I was resisting the external pressure. Mad as hell and holding breath for a long time. The original, "I won't." Breathing felt like an externally imposed defeat. In other sessions I had felt I was defeating the therapy process by breathing too soon. Finally this feeling of defeat made sense in terms of birth. Long sobbing. Then Christina asked, "What is your right hand doing?" It was in a fist. I explored this and it became rage, but with an important difference. This time it was rage with breathing. Looking back I can see that anger with held breath, clenched jaw and tight throat is a common pattern for me. Rage incompletely expressed.

Figure 6—Female Demon Dream

September 14, 1977

A half-waking dream of being clutched by a huge black female insane demon, who is lying on top of me. Sexual arousal, feeling drugged and unable to move. A membrane stretched over me, trapping me. (*See Figure 6*) Intense pain in right knee. The demon is also panicked. I want the demon to go away, not sure where I am, not sure why I don't let go to orgasm. Someone on the other side of the membrane pokes a hole in it, and I stick my tongue through. I awoke with my mouth open and nose and sinuses blocked. Shaken and amazed. It was clearly a perinatal dream. I want to draw and paint it. It relates to the first part of the dream of Mother raping me.

Stan said the membrane was the amniotic sac.

September 17, 1977

I want the feeling of union without requiring physical contact with another body. There was a moment of oneness with everything around me just as I started to jog this morning. This body had been just the jogging aspect of something much larger which was all me. The naming of it to myself instituted the split again, but there *was* that one moment of consciously experienced union.

September 22, 1977   Work with a friend

Aware of being a new possibility, not having the dynamic of vaginal birth imprinted in me. No beaten path to follow. Responsive to each new stimulus. Making love with the universe. Image of "me-ness" oozing in and out among rows of bottles and instruments. The operating room?

Energy changes. I feel cut open, great wound in my belly. Was I, as a newborn, still merged in consciousness with my cut-open mother lying on the operating table? Images of guts and raw meat being eaten by chickens. No emotion. Fiery sensations that would be pain if I resisted them.

October 17, 1977   Dream

I am with a man, working on breathing. I want to use a chest respirator he has. He's surprised but willing. He turns it on, and as he slips it over my head I start to suffocate and panic. Then he pulls it down, and it breathes for me. I feel very secure, body comfortable and energized.

December 14, 1977

Three people massaged me at once in a class. I experienced my flesh merging with them. Became a beautiful, cared-for baby. Because the class was almost over, they stopped abruptly and moved on to someone else, leaving me open and alone. I felt abandoned. I wished they had stayed with me and let me separate at my own speed. It wasn't until today that I became aware of what I had felt.

Too often in groups, I have felt hurt when the arbitrary structure of the sessions has taken precedence over my inner timing. So much pain from being forced too soon.

January 14, 1978

Stan asked me if I had any sense of direction about my work with him. My honest answer would have been no. Instead of saying that, I talked about a few superficial things. But the sense of aimlessness is real. Somehow this aimlessness is judged to be wrong by me and by others. I often make up stories and create melodramas in order not to be aimless and thus wrong. I remember what Stan once said about non-labor caesareans having no goals and being criticized for this. Perhaps the way out of this bind is to let it be OK both to have goals and not to have goals.

Chapter 3

Air: Ideas and More Adventures

About halfway through this period of living in Mendocino and following my inner journey with the support of workshops with the Grofs, I began to think of sharing what I was learning. I realized this was more than my personal journey. I saw that a record of my explorations might be helpful to other caesarean-born people. I began to write down my ideas, as well as to record my experiences.

I began to use the mental, air element of my being. Fire and water continued to be present in dreams and in further explorations of emotion.

January 18, 1978

A caesarean *world-view*—a different way of entering the world. I am interested in how the world appears to caesarean-born people. Does this world-view show in art by caesarean-born people? I think of my photos and paintings. What are the characteristics of a caesarean world-view?

I want to be aware of any tendency to view caesarean birth as better or worse than vaginal birth. I simply see it as different.

How to reconcile the apparent experience of being "done to" with my intuitive sense of being responsible for my life. For me this has something to do with the concept of separateness, of boundaries, of self-image, of what I mean by "I."

Of what value is defining a caesarean world-view? To caesarean-born people? To parents of caesarean-born people? To society in general?

To what extent are patterns of vaginal birth that are manifest in personality and in culture shown up in greater clarity by caesarean born patterns?

On a cosmic level, how does the increasing number of caesarean-born people manifest a shift in the karma, in the energy patterns, of the world as a whole?

Is this simply the latest manifestation of God (or Self) playing games? A new experiment?

January 23, 1978

I feel an ambivalence about this project. The caesarean thing seems to be difference and unlimited possibility. To generalize about it does violence to its very nature. It is the first step toward an orthodox view of the unorthodox. Yet these ideas are emerging in myself and in others, and I'd prefer that a caesarean-born person rather than a non-caesarean-born person do the naming. I am aware that I'm as much creating something called a caesarean world-view as I am discovering something that is already there. Yet it begins to be clear this is true even in what is supposed to be the most objective of sciences—physics. In my Ph.D. thesis, did I create, or did I discover, a split energy level in the "S" recurrence of the A_2 meson?

Caesareans are different. Caesareans are also not different. I want to find a balance between these two positions, appreciating the difference without being attached to it.

January 27, 1978

Awoke at 1 a.m. I tried meditating. Immediately the left side of my face felt huge, without boundaries. There followed a long period of allowing, like awake-dreaming. It was non-verbal and non-visual, all body awareness. Breathing emerged as an entity, along with a lot of emotion. "They were more interested in 'breathing' than they were in me." This probably is in connection with birth and drowning. Lots of anger toward "breathing." It became clear I had directed this anger toward men who take interest in my breathing, such as Dick, Paul and Stan. I associate breathing with a gigantic interruption in my inner process by an intrusion from the outside. I became aware of my chest, throat and face as a battleground of "me" vs. "breathing." There is a dead area in the middle, a layer of tension on the "front line," a body manifestation of the deep inner split. I thought of the sense of defeat I felt in work with Stan and Christina early in the September workshop, when I let go and allowed breathing after a long, choking holding. Breath came with a sense of being defeated. I also think of the chest respirator and suffocation dream in October.

This is part of a pattern of disowning breath. I must have integrated it enough to survive but wasted great amounts of energy fighting it within my body. As I continued to explore I felt a bit more acceptance of breathing.

Such a discovery. The hated interruption was from within as well as from without. I fell asleep after this quite easily. Then a dream, and such a dream. Remembering it brought a lot of softness into my face and my breathing.

The dream: I am in a house near a pond formed by an earthen dam. It has been raining a lot, and much water is flowing in the stream. There is a white wooden footbridge across the pond.

I decide to cross the bridge. My weight starts to sink the boards into the water. I notice a section of the bridge ahead is missing; the whole bridge is floating west toward a sturdier road bridge. I decide to climb onto the road bridge. But it, too, begins to disintegrate, so I try to cross on the dam itself. I see a large rock fall out of the dam, then another, and some water. I realize the dam itself is disintegrating. I run back toward the house, yelling, "The dam has broken!"

I am full of excitement and have no fear. I can't run as fast as I want to. I know the people in the house won't be affected by the flood, but I wish I could warn the people downstream. The people in the house and I go to see the flood. It is magnificent. Immense power. The water looks like a big muscular arm. It is beautiful and not destructive. I point out that we have our valley back. The grass meadow that was under the pond isn't dead; it is yellowish and scruffy looking, but clearly it will grow back. A small stream runs down its center.

This dream was an affirmation of the opening, flow and release of obstruction I had experienced during the night.

As I explored more, I began to be less judgmental of my journey as being weird or crazy. This first time I talked about my experience with another non-labor caesarean-born person was a powerful experience of mutual affirmation.

February 1, 1978
My caesarean-born friend said, "We're different. We had no boundaries. I always felt my head wasn't connected with my body." She asked if I knew how they pulled us out. She said, "Like this," and put her thumb in her mouth, pulling up against her hard palate. She said her father watched the operation and told her this. She also had a near-drowning. Hearing this affirmed my feeling that the near-drowning was a repeat of the birth dynamic.

When I showed her my painting of an old woman holding a lantern in a cave and spoke of wanting to go into the light, she said she, too, felt an attraction toward the inner light, a sense of forgetting her body. Once, in guided fantasy, she went into the light. It had taken the help of her friends and a bath to bring her back. She also spoke of rigidly holding her head. This was a valuable exchange for us, meeting a sister, validating each other.

February 2, 1978
I see a connection between a caesarean's apparent lack of goals and Taoist emphasis on being, rather than on doing or achieving.

February 12, 1978
Reading poetry by a friend who was born caesarean. I was struck by images of cold, ice and cutting in his poetry.

A midwife friend says many caesarean-born babies are angry at birth. They seem to be fighting the interruption.

March 7, 1978
Attitudes of caesarean-born people toward having children. I don't want to perpetuate my experience of what life is or pass on this way of being. A caesarean-born friend said he'd felt the same. It took several years of marriage before he agreed to have children.

March 20, 1978   Working alone
Aware that it is my positive feelings toward Stan I suppress the most.
The feeling of wanting to melt into him, to go into the love. Afraid that this
will be criticized, called transference or dependence, made not OK.
Chose to go into the positive anyhow. Images and sensations of melting
into Stan's warm, brown stomach. Felt myself regress into baby
consciousness. Then there was no longer any sense of either him or of me.
Just images and sensations that I can best describe as cellular
consciousness. Not his cells or my cells, just cells. Then quite quickly, all
this changed to a sense of being out in the galaxies. I was one with all of it.

March 22, 1978
I did a painting of a baby inside the belly of a being that is a mix of warm,
brown bear/Aztec priest/Stan. Fantasized it giving birth to me vaginally.
Much fear and resistance. Image of Stan giving birth to me in our working
sessions, both in terms of intense contact and in the sense of one adult
giving a gift to another. Didn't go all the way through this, too scary.

March 24, 1978
I see my uncertainty about the strong positive feelings I have toward
Stan and Christina. These are even harder to deal with than the negative
ones. Easy to feel that they are more wrong. Yet every time I allow them
fully in fantasy, I quickly transcend the personal level and come into these
same feelings in a more universal sense.

March 22, 1978
Stan pointed out that caesarean birth hasn't been studied by psychiatry
as much as the minutest details of toilet training. He suggested that
perhaps caesarean birth was too horrible for people to want to examine.
Perhaps so. Yet birth in general is only now being studied. The lack of
interest in caesarean birth is probably partly from the assumption that
people don't remember birth.

*In 1974 and 1975, there were three clear instances of my noticing a
pattern of physical and emotional energy in another person. I felt it was
something I hadn't seen often and that it was also like a physical and
emotional pattern in myself. In all three cases the person was in a stressful
social situation. There seemed to be a lot of fear, terror even. There was
physical shaking they tried to control, and there seemed to be tightness
between the shoulder blades in the center of the back. I found out all three
had been born non-labor caesarean. I realized I might be looking at
something characteristic of caesareans. The following conversation with
a friend was the first time I had heard anyone else speak of this.*

March 22, 1978

A friend told me of comments about caesareans made at a seminar. The people spoke of two kinds of response to stimulus—primitive fight/flight, which is an all or nothing response, and a more refined response that can judge subtle differences among stimuli, such as what is intended by another person who makes touch contact. These two are apparently integrated in the intense encounter of vaginal birth. They said this integration doesn't happen in caesareans, leaving them much more at the mercy of the fight/flight response. They spoke of some neurological research that showed this. I recognized this as a description of much that I've experienced and recognized in other caesareans.

My friend spoke about a spot on the back between the shoulder blades. That's the spot where I've felt so much happening. In a dream, I was touched there. In exploring that dream with Natalie, she touched me there. When I fully allowed myself to feel the touch, it brought me to letting go totally and feeling newborn. I spoke of this place to a caesarean-born friend the next day and she exclaimed, "That's my spot!" She said that much of her inner work has centered there, too. I was excited about finding some hint of physiological basis for what I experience, and I was sad at the many times I have pushed away contact because of this fight/flight response. It is one of the major ways I have isolated myself and created misunderstanding with other people. My friend also spoke of caesareans wanting intense contact experiences. This, too, fits.

March 27, 1978

Ambivalence. Not sure if I want to be here or not. A baby pulled into the world and not quite agreeing to the process. The ambivalence is positive, a very centered place.

Separation. As an archetype perhaps. Necessary for the emergence of something new, something untouched—here I mean "touch" on many levels. The theme of separation seems to be strong in the caesarean born, though by no means unique to them. The separation created space for something different to form, something outside the mainstream culture. When it is discovered by the mainstream, it may be devoured, changed and perverted.

I am not sure I want to name all these things, to expose the secrets of the caesarean world, many of which are unconscious to most caesareans even. Afraid the exposure will destroy the magic. Maybe what I want to do is just say to all caesareans, including myself, "We are not wrong or defective, just different."

April 5, 1978

Every intervention and limit by people I do inner work with seems to get tangled with the emotion I have about interruption. Every interruption threatens "me." Perhaps this is necessary. I need to become comfortable with letting "me" die, then allowing the creation of a new "me."

April 11, 1978   My birthday

More thoughts on boundaries, limits and freedom. I'm leaving this apartment because I get tense having to be so quiet for my landlady. Last night with her away, I came to understand how she was a limit for me, one I needed. As I begin to be conscious of creating my own limits, I need fewer external limits.

Last month I saw how over and over I have torn myself out of comfortable situations. I imagined a hostile world "out there," and behaved accordingly, thus creating exactly what I expected. I begin to do this differently.

I see myself transforming the dynamics that might come from birth. I still like being able to tolerate great pressure, sudden change and lack of definition. What is important is that I now see that these are things I do, rather than "how the world is," which is what they had always seemed to be.

April 13, 1978

A dream. As intense as the female demon dream last September and the chest respirator dream last October. All three were body dreams and felt almost more real than my waking reality.

The dream: I'm with a group of people at Stan and Christina's house. I'm sitting on a couch with my back to the ocean. I become withdrawn, lying curled up. One by one the people leave until I'm alone with Stan and Christina. I'm anxious, afraid it's not OK for me to be there.

Stan and Christina ask how I'm doing and touch me. I start to cry loudly and cling to them. I am afraid they'll think I manipulated them and will be angry with me, but I take the risk. They hold me and encourage me to feel whatever is happening. I shake and cry. I feel like I'm disintegrating. I fall off the couch. They stay with me, still holding me and pushing on me with their hands. As I fall there is an intense pain in my lower back, which was arched backward. They continue to help with contact and encouraging words. My neck is arched backward. I feel a popping across my throat. I imagine a string of beads that breaks under strain. I feel totally regressed, and am extremely glad of the intense full body contact Stan and Christina are giving me.

Waking up was the rough part. I was still regressed, crying baby cries, no adult consciousness, aware of contact with Stan and Christina. Then I saw my room and felt myself alone. I felt the warm supporting presence go away and the openness close down. I felt absolutely devastated. Sobbed. Strong sense of, "I don't want to be here."

Later I got a glimmer that "here" is only partly geographical. Part of it is an inner state of aloneness. Part of "there" is being with Stan and

Christina, and part of it, too, is an inner state of connectedness. It would be easy to try too soon to say the sense of openness and contact is within me, rather than dependent on external circumstances. All that is real for me so far is that one glimmer of connection. When I try too soon to say it is within, I create more tension by trying to suppress the feelings of loneliness, longing and devastation that are still very real. The birth-related self-constriction is not yet fully released.

April 17, 1978   Dream

There is a group of astronauts. Sometimes I'm one of them, and sometimes I'm an observer. Someone says that when the whirling starts, it is dangerous to be too far from the center. The forces would crush one. I hear what happens when the control computer program is changed, when a new flight-plan/life-support program is started. "The dangerous time is when the old program has been cancelled and the new one not started yet." A visual image of turning off one switch and turning on another. Feeling of a floating void, a stillness. The danger is that somehow the new program won't start, that one becomes lost, leaves the body and can't find the way back, dies. It is a time of great danger and also a time without the possibility of any action.

I had been using caesarean birth as a conceptual framework for about four years. I was allowing a lot to surface, but I wasn't sure how much change I was allowing. My intellectual fascination with the subject was in some ways a hindrance to my growth. It was becoming clear that my birth learning, which I had been so carefully mapping, needed to become simply one among many ways of living and being.

The astronaut dream was a message from my higher self that has perspective and knows the way. The dream was guidance in the process of releasing my birth learning without losing my body. In subsequent dreams and inner work the theme of transformation becomes more and more evident.

It is interesting the dream uses the image of "survival and navigation programs." Each of us did indeed survive our birth and has navigated thus far in life. So our birth learning is just such a program, but it is not the only possible program. The survival of life on earth may depend on our ability to release old programming and live in new ways.

June 6, 1978

Caesarean birth as a sudden enormous expansion coupled with a holding of breath. I think I experience reruns of this as "tripping out," a holding of breath accompanied by inner images, followed by a sudden return to the present, a release of breath, and a realization that I have been somewhere else for a while.

Boundaries. A difficulty in telling what is me and what is not me psychically. Inner tension that is "me trying to keep myself contained." A fear other people will feel intruded upon when I am with them. I think of the numerous times people have told me they feel observed by me. I often sense that I am reading their minds.

June 26, 1978

Today I will meet with a friend to talk about this project. He is a non-labor caesarean.

This noon I was depressed. Crying, realizing I am afraid of the meeting. I felt afraid of his needs, then of the blind violence I imagine could erupt. I thought of Tom Ednie's comment that caesareans probably don't experience what Kierkegaard calls the ethical realm, only the aesthetic realm which has no morality. Tom thinks the ethical realm corresponds to labor. I know the ruthlessness in myself, the sudden violence that scares people. Today I experienced both sides of this, the terror and the ruthlessness.

July 3, 1978

Today a friend's insistence on objectivity, separateness and boundaries created a familiar difficulty for me. I was having a hard time going along with the much more defined world of the vaginally born. I, too, know the state of definition, but it feels like a great effort to maintain it. It is not deeply rooted in me. It was learned bit by bit in social interaction, not in birth. It feels like denial of what I know to be my true identity, identity with everything.

I think of Stan saying that I seem to have had transpersonal experiences, but have negative associations with them. I get an image of people trying to stuff me back into the container they think is me. Only I keep leaking out, and they get scared because it threatens their boundaries and self-image. I feel relief about relaxing my great effort to maintain socially acceptable boundaries. There is a difference between caesareans and others in their position on the continuum between total separation and total oneness. Perhaps much of my fighting with the world is over boundaries. So many people say I demand too much. I have learned I am supposed to have boundaries, so I continually test where they are.

July 13, 1978

In the rape/murder/birthday dream I walked out of the room where all the violence was. I walked into the empty hall, from which I was free to go in any direction. I realize that I stay stuck emotionally by refusing to walk out and face being in the hall not knowing what is next.

I think of quitting this inner journey, of asking Stan if he is into being a cosmic garbage collector and giving him all my writings and drawings. A fantasy of selling or giving away all my possessions, wanting to go naked and start afresh. I'm aware an external stripping may not be to the point. An inner change is needed. For now I don't know what corresponds to walking out into the hall.

I'm uncomfortable, feeling there is nothing in the external world that interests me now—still—again. A fog is between me and the world. I want a soft place where I will be cared for. That want is between me and everything else.

July 1978   Work with Stan and Christina

A lot of emotion during the slide show of vaginal birth, especially at delivery. All the images of fire and breaking through. I despaired of ever being able to reach that kind of victory. Stan and Christina worked with me some. I felt chaos and confusion and judgment. Stan helped me to just experience the chaos, confusion, fragmentation and irrationality. Perhaps it is related to the anesthesia.

July 26, 1978

I met another caesarean in Stan's five-day workshop. I was first struck by the tense look on her face, like a sneer, an expression of disgust, of "no." At first I reacted by thinking I didn't like her. Then I recognized that look as a reflection of myself. She spoke of caesareans being undefended against the onslaught of stimulation that greets them at birth, because they haven't had the tactile and pressure stimulation of labor and delivery. She asked if I find caesareans have a high level of anxiety.

July 28, 1978

I decided to explore. I put a big pillow into a corner and pushed my head into it while on my hands and knees. Full soft contact on head, neck and shoulders. Much emotion. "This is what I have been wanting all along." I remembered Stan talking of how LeBoyer's baby massage reproduces the contact of the womb.

July 30, 1978

Last night, I got a strong urge to do some yoga, awareness work, and meditation. I felt something important was near the surface. I did a few stretches and felt a gentle opening. I was in transition between my ordinary world and an altered state of consciousness. I slowly came to stillness and a sense of delight. I spent a long time gently following awareness. Then an image of someone touching me and asking how I was doing. I imagined saying, "I think you want to help me." There emerged an image of a possible response, something about touch, letting go, disintegrating, no boundaries. In fantasy, I said, "I'm not ready yet to speak of what really was happening in response to your question and touch." I have a hard time even writing about what came next—cellular reality, graininess, light, dark, no space/time—not sure these words fit.

The next clear image was a memory of Dick touching me in a workshop three-and-a-half years ago. Re-experiencing what I felt then—total openness, love, oneness, energy moving through my body. Aware that I have trapped Dick in that memory. Then I had a sense of finally being able to separate my experience from my image of him.

The next image was a memory of Stan touching me. Sense of not knowing where I stopped and he started. Feeling his hand still there even after he had removed it. Remembering this, I again realized I'd held onto an image. What was him and what was me got mixed up in the separating; I had kept a visual image of the hand and attributed the sensation of the touch to him. The same confusion about boundaries and about what is who.

Then I had a clear memory of being bathed as a baby. There was a mixture of pleasant feelings and sensations, along with awareness of Mother's tension, anxiety, discomfort with touch.

All these experiences generalize into a speculation that my sense of me, my body image, my ego sense, is a conglomeration of my touch encounters, many of the contradictory and chaotic. When I fully allow touch, I merge with the other person physically, emotionally and mentally. I wonder if caesareans are more likely to experience this than those who experienced vaginal birth with its overwhelming tactile stimulation, which is a whole body experience and forms a filter for later touch experience. I think of a friend telling me with amazement that he felt me as being totally malleable when I lay next to him.

The other part of this dynamic is a general tensing against touch. Part of the fear of allowing myself to be touched deeply is the memory of repeated, insensitive, tearing separations. Touching is filled with highly charged ambivalence for me—the ecstasy of merging, the terror of the tearing, too-quick separation. Mostly I let the fear dominate. When I am in contact with another person, I participate in their coherence. I sense it as mine and let go of some rigidity, some defenses. After the experiences and thoughts described above, I fell asleep easily. I woke again, astounded at the following dream.

The Dream:

I am lying on a table. A doctor is about to perform a caesarean on me. He is using no anesthesia. I feel the pain only as sensation. He makes a vertical incision like the one Mother had, separating muscles rather than cutting across them. I feel him pushing on my belly as he gets the baby out. He pulls the baby free with the cord still attached. I reach down and pull it up to my breast where it sucks. It is a big baby, not clear which sex. It seems awake and aware. I hug the baby and say, "Your birthday is near mine. You're an Aries, too. I feel very close to you." I felt a lot of good fiery energy. I was surprised at how little tension I felt.

August 3, 1978   Dream (*See Figure 7*)

I am driving south on US 1 towards Boston. The air is bad—polluted or poisoned. A low plane flies over. I see a fire in a large office building that is unoccupied. Some workers are breaking through the gate in the fence around it. I crawl over, under, and through a tangle of hoses, then spray water on the building. I go into the building and find that it is a dormitory. I meet a professor friend there.

Another perinatal dream. I was born in Boston. The bad air is the anesthesia, the breaking in is the operation, the tangle of hoses is the umbilical cord and the dormitory is the nursery.

Figure 7—Boston Dream

August 1978

Through some strange coincidences, a man travelling through here with his girlfriend spent an evening visiting me. He said he was born non-labor caesarean. This made sense of the intensity I had felt in conversation with him. He had a way of pushing on and on until I explicitly set limits. His girlfriend said she was delighted to see how well I handled him, how I called his number over and over.

He wasn't angry with me. Rather, he seemed pleased at being met. He told of a psychic to whom he went for a reading. Her first question to him was, "Do you do this to everyone you meet?" Puzzled, he asked, "Do what?" She answered that she felt him probing her mind. Perhaps an expanded state of awareness is so normal for caesareans that they don't even recognize it as such, and only have negative associations with it, those of other people feeling intruded upon.

August 5, 1978

A dream after talking of my fear and depression with a friend last night. She suggested we each dream about it. It worked. Falling asleep I told myself my body was safe and that whatever I needed to experience in dream was OK.

The dream: I'm on a steep mountainside. It is winter, cloudy and about to snow more. Some friends have gone off somewhere. I have taken a drug. It feels right to be alone. I lie down and let myself slide rapidly down through the powdery snow. I let go completely. Feels like something I have wanted to do for a long time. Then I think about the bottom and panic. I'm afraid I'll crash. Images of fire, crushing and pain. Fear of death. I begin to clutch frantically to stop the sliding. Breathing becomes difficult. Eventually I lie there terrified. I feel like I'm buried in piles of soft snow. I begin to climb back up the hill. The I hear a knock on the door and my friend saying, "You decided to come back." I'm in the stairwell of my childhood elementary school, only it is much deeper than three stories. I see my friend behind a glass firedoor a ways above me.

Then I woke up. I was aware of great tension. It is clear that I want to totally let go, but I'm afraid of dying. I am afraid I can choose to die by choosing to let go, even without water to drown in, maybe the way old Indian people are said to die. Last night's dream was, however, a step in releasing this fear.

This dream is related to the experience of anesthesia and to the "Ether Demon" and his snowy mountains. (See May 14, 1977.) The resolution of the fear of dying came several years later not in relation to my caesarean birth experience, but with re-living and releasing what appears to have been a past-life death. This was one area where the concept of birth-learning was too limited to be useful. Stan Grof was correct in placing birth between childhood memory (like my near-drowning experience) and transpersonal realms (of which past life-recall is an example). Each conceptual framework is useful in the appropriate area of the psyche.

November 1978

Some thoughts on the tension between Dick and me. I sense that the doctor who pulled me out of my mother tried to get me to breathe by pushing on my chest. I think I reacted to him with terror, anger and resistance. Dick's pushing on my chest as we worked brought up all that emotion. Somehow I didn't connect it back to birth, but projected it onto the present, creating a lot of tension between us.

I seem to have later let go of the resistance and merged with that doctor and felt great love for him. He probably thought he was starting my breathing with his hands. It is more likely that I learned to breathe by attuning to his breathing and to his whole being, experiencing this as total orgasm. The bond with my mother was broken. I bonded with him and then felt totally shattered when he, too, left me. I think unconsciously I have been reliving this pattern with men ever since.

Chapter 4
Seeds of Transformation

In November 1978, I moved to San Francisco and lived with a family that had been part of a community I lived in from 1971 to 1973. That provided a safe place in which to continue my inner journey while reconnecting more with the world.

One motivation for the move was to study with Angeles Arrien and with Ralph Metzner, both of whom I had met during the Grofs' month-long workshop at Esalen. I felt their knowledge of expanded, transpersonal states of consciousness and of applying this to ordinary concerns would be helpful to me.

I learned that intellect and concept are tools, rather than ways to control and explain reality. My inner journey and insights about caesarean birth continued, but in a more subdued fashion. It was a time of incubation and taking in new resources. Perhaps I was planting seeds in the ground I had plowed and prepared in the preceeding years.

January 15, 1979
Exploring what "dependency" is for me. Still aware of fear of being rejected. Yet hidden within "dependency" is something positive—a dissolving of boundaries. Maybe this is the pearl to be taken from the clingy, clutchy dependency demon.

January 19, 1979   Dream
I am lying in a small bedroom. I have been asleep. Everything starts shaking and moving in unfamiliar, unpredictable ways. Thoughts of an earthquake. I feel drugged and can't move. Want to get out into the trees. A man's voice in an adjacent, larger room says, "This is it." I am scared. Tight in chest. I can't get to the trees. Then somehow I am in the next room. End of dream. So clearly about birth!

This dream came while I was taking a class with Angeles Arrien, a native-born Basque. She said that among Basques who maintain their mystical tradition, some births occur in nature rather than in buildings. She can remember her own birth in nature. I wonder if in this dream I was remembering both my caesarean birth and a birth in nature from a previous lifetime.

February 13, 1979

From page 296 of *Brain Revolution* by Marilyn Ferguson:
"Observation, acute sensory perception, plays a role in the creative personality. According to one study, there is a strong correlation between the sensory threshold of infants and their later imaginative tendencies. Those relatively insensitive when tested at a few months of age were later inclined to center their play around concrete objects, whereas low-threshold infants later tended to talk about imaginary playthings and imaginary companions."

What is real and what is imaginary? I think that distinction probably approximates the sensory threshold of "normal" people. People whose sensing is more acute are said to be imagining things. People aware of transpersonal realms also would be said to be imagining things. I connect this to comments about caesareans being "tactile defensive," "special" and more easily in touch with transpersonal realms. "Normal" sensory thresholds might be those of the vaginally born.

Studying a transpersonal perspective on reality has helped me affirm that rather than being a beginning point, birth may be a transition from one reality to another. The boundaries between these realms, rather than being absolutes, are more like cultural conventions.

March 1, 1979

Last night I looked at the drawing of caesarean birth I did for Angie's class. Then I saw it just as it is—mother out of it with anesthesia and the doctor supporting a shining, new person. I saw this dependence without judging it. There may be a way out of the fear of dependence after all.

March 12, 1979

I awoke with an intense dream image: A baby bottle tilted, nipple down, filled with water or a pale juice. In it, there is a baby drowning. (*See Fig. 8*)

This dream seems to be about the anesthesia. I may have experienced a lack of oxygen that felt like drowning. The baby bottle is perhaps the uterus, and the fluid the amniotic fluid.

After I awoke, I lay in bed shivering, feet very cold. Intense fear of dying if I let go. There seems to be something I must not let happen when I'm alone, with no one to rescue me.

With each teacher I face a little more of the fear, become less dependent, do a little more of giving birth to myself. That evening after drawing the birth situation, an acceptance emerged. Yes, I was supported and rescued, and that is OK. The importance of accepting that situation is that then I am not so likely to keep repeating it compulsively. I have so much ambivalence about support, dependence and help. There is such a fine line between helping someone unfold, become more fully themselves, trusting them, or giving the kind of "help" that stifles growth.

Figure 8—Bottle Dream

May 27, 1979

I began to think of my caesarean work last night and became negative. I felt cheated, angry, not really here. Memory of wanting to cling to Dick and to Stan and of having suppressed that want. Fantasy of a large body to cling to.

After wanting to cling, I became aware that the next thing that tries to happen might be violent. I asked four fantasy people to hold my wrists and ankles while I lay on my back. What followed surprised me. I discovered the feeling of clinging flips over into intense desire to kill. My fear had been well founded. If a person was comforting me as I flipped over into the violence, I might well have hurt him or her. Deep sobbing followed the murderous rage. I released much fear and terror through the sobbing. Feelings of love emerged. Next came a sense that, perhaps in another incarnation, there had been violence between Dick and me.

Lying there, I was aware that the next step was to re-own my hands and feet. I began to feel tingling in my hands and feet as I moved awareness into them. Aware of a changed body image, arms especially feeling more part of me. Frog image! Laughter came. New openness in chest where the fear had been. Felt tingling sensations in my body. A burning feeling in the soles of my feet, different from the pain of blocked energy. I let the process of energy movement continue into sleep. This morning I awoke with an amazing dream that shows the positive transformation and the fiery energy.

The dream: On a beach, the sun is low. I sit with a group of people. Dick is leaning on my left leg. I am glad he feels comfortable with me. Then we run and dance along the beach, making loops and wiggles, like skiing. Ecstasy. I notice my shadow. The two sides are dark. There is yellow/white light up the middle of the torso and through the middle of the head. Dick's shadow is similar. I say, "Look at all the light in my heart." (*See Figure 9*)

Figure 9—Lighted Shadows

I seem to have avoided writing down anything of my black negativity last June, when I was seeing caesarean birth as a disaster, a gyp. I was angry at having been dumped into the world without labor and delivery as a prototype for relationship.

The same blackness arose last night. This time I stopped judging it, and out of the blackness emerged the inner work and the dream of the lighted shadow.

The other side of the sense of having been gypped out of a proper birth is the sense of having been greedy, of having tried a shortcut. I was full of guilt at having tried to come into the world without going through all that vaginal birth involved. Despair, feeling that suicide was the only way out, that I should go back out and come in properly, not avoiding vaginal birth. I have been in this state several times. The way out of it seems to go into a quiet, non-thinking awareness of the present or to fall asleep. Fighting the guilt and despair only makes it worse. Acceptance is what transforms the situation.

Tonight I read through all I've written on caesarean birth. Something has changed inside me since facing the darkness. I feel more detached and clear about this material. I now need to structure it into a readable form. A midwife friend spoke of the needs of the mothers of caesarean babies. Perhaps I can help. I laugh at how much I resisted reading all this. I was remembering the old conflicts and was not aware that many of them are resolved now.

June 2, 1979

Some thoughts on what Stan has said about ego death in relation to birth, about the necessity of surrender to something larger than one's self, and on what I read by a woman who planned for natural childbirth and had a caesarean delivery: "Those of us who are supportive of natural childbirth tend to put incredible expectations on ourselves. I had so many high expectations of what I was capable of doing and how I would do it. My expectations were the hardest things to deal with." In the same article is the following quote, "Drs. Arthur and Libby Colman, in their book, *Pregnancy: The Psychological Experience*, write: 'Almost all women see labor and delivery as a test of their womanhood. They want to be proud of what has happened.' Can the woman who has had a caesarean birth feel as if she has failed some test?"

Is the increase in caesarean deliveries among women who had planned natural childbirth perhaps a result of too much ego attachment to the accomplishment of giving birth? The little self, the "I," wants to "do" the birth, and this prevents the surrender, the ego death that is a normal part of birth, that allows the larger Self to do what it does with wisdom. This seems likely to me. In a caesarean, the larger Self gets its way ultimately, forcing a surrender, not to the body wisdom of the mother, but to the doctors and the clinical procedure. Unless the mother can somehow let go of enough of her individual self-image to know her unity with these "other" people, she sees the caesarean as a defeat, rather than seeing it as the triumph of a Self that has several physical bodies. This identifying with a larger Self, that includes baby, mother and doctor, has been the only way out of a sense of defeat for me as the baby. Perhaps it is also the only way out of a sense of failure and defeat for the mother. Caesarean birth seems to be of a transpersonal nature both for the mother and for the baby.

June 2, 1979

More thoughts on "ego formation" in the birth process. I imagine that a self-image is formed in the womb, an image that is based on living there for nine months. The self-image may be almost totally physical and sensual, existing in muscular tensions.

Labor and delivery change all this. In order to come out physically through the birth canal, all tension must be released; one is "oozed out"; this is ego death. Then there is space for a new ego to form, one that is appropriate to living in a separate physical body.

Caesareans don't experience such a complete loss of their self-image and perhaps retain some of the "in the womb" personality. Perhaps this is what Stan refers to when he says caesareans feel unborn. This has positive and negative aspects. One retains the "good womb" image of the world but perhaps doesn't have all the tools for dealing with separate physical existence.

Is there a parallel for mothers of caesareans? An incomplete letting go of the "pregnant lady" self-image? Most initiation processes have two stages—a death of the old and a birth of the new.

Figure 10—"This is Caesarean Birth" Dream

July 27, 1979   Dream (See Figure 10)
I am at a seminar. A male leader tells a small group an account of a process. Mostly he speaks of what the person involved would experience. I felt the process was scary. Some details I saw happen to a small naked person; others I experienced as happening to me. Being grabbed by the head. Hearing the man say, "And we do it like this." Pulled by head backward. Being arched forcefully back. Pain and resistance in my chest. The group is horrified. Then the leader says, "And this is caesarean birth." I experience a great flood of emotion. He has been using me as an example.

Then we are in a plowed field. I am lying on the ground on my right side. The group leader is now a large man with golden hair. We are both naked. He lies on top of me, pressing me into the earth. I experience and release all the hurt, fear and anger I'd felt in the birth. A healing. I feel awe and gratitude. Later I am in the same field replanting some uprooted beets. Someone asks what group I'd been in. I describe what I experienced. I feel I am not communicating well. Later, I am riding in a car with a friend. She belittles my experience. I feel hurt.

July 30, 1979

Awakening from a dream: Lying on my belly, not sure if I am breathing right, can't move, people poking me, I can't communicate. Sense of suffocation, letting it be, no fear. Was this a dream? Perhaps I was reliving being a newborn—not strong enough to breathe, still full of ether, can't roll over.

August 1979

I wonder if birth influences the dynamics of relationship. I tend to be direct, all or nothing, like an arrow. Do the vaginally born relate with an ebb and flow, like waves of labor contractions?

August 21, 1979

A dream: Coming to a gathering of people, feeling tired and drained, not liking the clothes I am wearing. At the door are my parents. They hug me. I start to cry and to merge with them.

Remembering this dream, I felt a lot of resistance. I don't want to merge with them. A lot of fear. I went into the feelings while staying in touch with a source of light and clarity. I experienced more about boundaries, about depending on Mother to set boundaries, thinking of the "labor" we never did. Then came a positive playing with soft boundaries, probably in the womb. Abrupt change to jerking and arching, then lying still, quiet and tentative. I went through this sequence twice, each time entering body more. Not mad at world, more sense of not being hurried, of having time.

August 28, 1979

I've wanted various lovers and therapists to give birth to me. I mean that I've wanted them to relate to me as an equal in a situation where there are no rules. Labor is that kind of situation. There are no mental rules; the body is the only rule. I'm so tired of trying to meet expectations about relationship.

September 14, 1979

I've been subconsciously caught up in birth energies for a long time. As they surface, I tend to act them out more. The situation can get rather precarious. Being conscious of this is good.

I thought of asking Stan if he'd ever worked with a caesarean who he felt had fully re-experienced and transcended birth. I imagined his answer would be no. I realized I've been assuming he knows the whole pattern, and I had been angry he wasn't sharing it with me. After this, I saw him as an equal, a fellow explorer.

October 7, 1979

Is it possible that "transpersonal" and "personal" have different meanings for caesarean-born than for vaginally-born people? Perhaps there is lack of communication when these words are used. The sense of personal boundaries is different. The "normal" culturally accepted ego boundaries may be unconsciously patterned after vaginal birth.

October 10, 1979   Work with a friend

I trust this friend in a special way because she is also non-labor caesarean. I went straight to the issue of contact and separation. I spoke of how I am afraid to open to anyone, not because the contact is scary, but because I'm afraid the separation will be painful. She was willing to let me merge with her and learn to separate without pain; she wasn't afraid of my becoming dependent. I cuddled up to her and put my head on her stomach. Merging, feeling safe. I don't know how long we lay there.

Eventually I moved away, aware the pain and longing were still there. I asked if I could try again. She said, "This time, lift your head last." I got on all fours, without lifting my head, and backed away. I experienced a few moments of something new—feeling connected while physically separate. I said, "Everything is going to be different after this." This experience was a first taste of something that becomes more and more how I am.

May 18, 1980

Caesarean birth as a "different doorway," a different way of coming in, and a different filter or set of illusions to transcend. Caesarean and vaginal birth offer each other contrasts, in the same way that knowledge of another culture gives one perspective on one's own culture. Because of the differences at the personal and biological levels between caesarean-born and vaginally-born people, they are forced to go deeper to find a common ground at the transpersonal level.

July 2, 1980   Meditation session

Wanting to let go of tension, but I am afraid of what might happen afterward. Images of people who are angry with me. The terrible tension and sense of separateness are intolerable. I feel rage toward the world, despair. Preferring to let go, even if it means dying. Understanding I can't go back into union with Mother, but not liking the separation, a dry, lifeless existence. I would rather give up my physical being than feel separate.

Then a glimmer of a new possibility. Realization that is is not the physical union I need. I need a unitive state of consciousness, an inner sense of being one with everything and everyone. I had this in the womb in conjunction with physical union. Physical separation doesn't have to mean psychic separation. The latter is an attitude I can hold or let go of, not something that was done to me as the physical part was. This experience of union is very tentative, lots of fear and denial still.

The need for union was behind my desperate attachments to a whole string of people and my deep desire for touch.

September 7, 1980

Thinking about Stan saying caesarean people feel the pressure, but they don't know they can push through it. Part of me said no to this. I was resisting being put into the mold of vaginal birth—the pushing through. I don't like the implication that vaginal birth is right and caesarean is a "problem." Then a possibility emerges of a different kind of action. It is neither the aggressive action of labor nor the helpless inaction of caesarean birth. An action that does not create an inner split between subject and object. A moment of transcending the patterns of both kinds of birth.

September 14, 1980

"Caesarean birth" is not limited in time to the removal of the baby from the mother. It continues for years. That caesareans appear "unborn" is one manifestation of this. Their births are still in process.

"Birth" on the physical level for a caesarean is much quicker than for the vaginally born. But paradoxically, caesarean birth also can be seen as taking much longer. Many physiological, psychological and maybe even spiritual processes that occur in labor and delivery for the vaginally born happen for caesareans, if they happen at all, in their encounters with the world and with people. Examples of this might be tactile stimulation, stimulation of other physiological systems, formation of ego boundaries and full acceptance of incarnation, of embodiment.

The idea of "birth" not being limited to the actual delivery also is found among the Basque people who consider the first seven year of life to be "birth." The perspective of seeing birth as an ongoing process may be appropriate for all births, although possibly more pronounced for caesareans.

As I wrote this, I recalled a dream from a couple of years ago, in which a friend and I sang a beautiful song together. "You must first be born; your freedom is innate." At the time of the dream, I sensed that it meant that I hadn't finished being born.

September 21, 1980

One obvious difference between caesarean and vaginal birth is that, in the latter, the head is pushed into the body during labor and delivery. In a caesarean delivery, often the baby is pulled out by the head. Various massage, tai chi and yoga practices involve stretching the neck or pulling on the head. This may help to release tension that has its roots in vaginal birth. I hold a lot of tension in my neck, but the usual neck extension practices do not release it for me. I notice more release when I allow my head to settle onto my neck and shoulders more firmly, or I push my head gently against something, or someone gently pushes my head into my body while I lie on my back very relaxed.

In the many therapies and spiritual practices I have experienced, I have usually found some helpful things but have always run into parts that feel wrong. I wonder if perhaps all these practices are designed unconsciously to deal with patterns of tension that are, in part, reflections of the vaginal birth process. I want to create some new practices that suit my own needs.

September 22, 1980

With caesarean birth, parents, doctors and babies choose to do consciously what has been done unconsciously or "naturally" in vaginal birth. The caesarean-born person is stimulated and given boundaries outside the mother's body, rather than in the trip down the birth canal. People other than mothers now share some of the "labor."

September 29, 1980

In pyschophysiology class today, Ralph spoke of the evolutionary increase in brain size being limited by the size of the maternal pelvic opening. I realized that caesarean births often are done because the baby's head is too big. Now the larger-brained babies, who would have died in birth, can survive and reproduce. Caesarean birth is allowing continued evolutionary increase in brain size!

October 17, 1980

Aware of holding onto my head with neck muscles. I think of how I continually give my head away, how I let someone else's conceptual framework act as mine, and how I carry around a visual image of their head.

Last night I allowed the holding in my neck to intensify. Lifting my head off the pillow and holding it as long as I could. A sense of having allowed my head to be held, clearly connected with birth. Letting the head pop out without fighting it, then intense holding when they pulled on my head. Body trying to remain in the womb, while head is out in the world. Intense emotion. A sense I had been afraid I was being killed. Some releasing and crying. My breathing was erratic and changing.

Muscles in my upper chest that should move with breath are usually immobilized by being part of the pattern of holding head and body together. This connects to the release I felt when Natalie pushed in on my head. Her pushing freed those muscles to participate in breathing. I lay here in my bed a while with my head pushed gently against a pillow. Some of the same release happened. Waves of energy and release moved down through my body. I stopped the process when one wave moved through my pelvis and I began to pee.

After the period of conceptualizing, I again moved into physical and emotional processing. This particular experience is perhaps connected with having for a time been holding ideas in my head. I had let my head, my ideas, once again move too fast for the rest of my being, just as it had in birth. Several months later the same opening deepened and became more integrated. It was another turn on the spiral of growth, coming back again and again to the same material, each time with more awareness.

March 3, 1981

Bored, restless. Afraid. A sense of not having done something I was supposed to do. Aware of it as a constant underlying terror I feel. "If you don't. . . ., I will kill you." Not knowing what ". . . ." is. Aware now that this voice is coming from within, not from the outside any more. Thoughts that I was "making all this up." Allowing the sense of making it up. Remembering that the point of this kind of process work is to experience consciously how I create these dynamics. When fully experienced, the pattern becomes optional and can be released. Feeling my response to that, "If you don't. . ." voice as the root of much of my constant need to be doing.

Trying to allow images. A few thoughts of birth or drowning. Then "If you don't. . . .you will die." Still no image for ". . . ." Free floating need to *do*. Sensation and movement in neck and upper chest. Then, "If you don't breathe, you will die." Then, "I don't want to breathe." Each breath a defeat. Aware that this is a more integrated version of work with Stan and Christina in September 1977. Becoming more aware of the threatening voice as part of me. Locked into the non-movement in chest and neck. Gentle releasing as all this becomes conscious.

Then, with a breath, there was a re-alignment of a vertebra above the area between my shoulder blades. A sense of gentle energy flow to new places. Openness in upper chest, the same as in work with Dick in December 1974 on "sad/moving," only now arrived at much more gently and on my own. Terror is gone. I feel quiet; I decide to write. Slow re-entry. Opening eyes, seeing without feeling I have to do anything. Some falling back into habitual tension while writing. Noticing it, then feeling vertebra re-align again.

Again, inner work emerged after a day of outer work on caesarean birth. I spent several hours yesterday at UC Med Center Library. I was aware of feeling unsettled by pictures of caesarean birth.

March 9, 1981

Birth Poem

Snail squirming grey slime
Tail long in water
Forming
Unforming

Clear starlight silver shimmer
Soft fire above me

Breath exploding in fragments of light
Expanding to the limits of the universe
Disintegrating
Dying

Heavy stone
Holding me against the explosion of
Light & Touch & Sound & Breath
A cool still dark center

I am

March 13, 1981

Each morning's rising is like a rebirth. Again and again I take on the form "Jane." And again and again, I emerge too soon, full of resentment and conflict that I carry into my day. Or I lie in bed full of the same resentment and get up late feeling sluggish. Occasionally though, I lie there giving myself permission to be nothing and do nothing. Aware only of curiosity as to what, if anything, will finally move me to get up.

Today I did it differently. Awoke full of restlessness and conflict, "I should get up and meditate." Then an inspiration—meditate lying in bed. On back, no movement, no sleeping, set timer for 30 minutes. I did this. Noticing all the resistance without judging it or trying to overcome it. Much changed. By the end, even my feet and hands were awake; breath and gut were held less. I arose easily and happily after the bell. Giving myself a new kind of birth.

March 23, 1981

I got a phone call from Daddy. He was upset I haven't called or written since I heard Mother was bitten by a spider a month ago and was in the hospital with an infected leg. He said she is upset with me, too. I told him I hadn't called because I didn't know how to communicate what I felt about it. To me, it seemed like a positive event, a releasing of all the fears she has had about spiders all her life. Her worst fear had happened, and she had survived. I said I was open to talking with her now. He asked her, and she said no.

Afterward, I was amazed at how happy I felt. I realized it was because, finally, she had done what she never did in the birth. She pushed me out! What a gift.

April 18, 1981

Natalie spoke of a child being "with God" before birth and agreeing to form and limitations at birth. This is part of the fascination newborns have for us—just a few moments before, they were "with God." A caesarean-born child is interrupted before having a chance to agree with this change. Natalie saw the people bringing gifts in my 1973 dream as an image of seduction, saying to the child, "Be with us for a while. It's not all bad. See, you can play with these beautiful toys."

Many times and in many ways people have tried to tell me it was OK to be here, though often they weren't aware this was what they were trying to do. Usually I rejected the demanding way in which they approached me, and along with this, their subconscious real message of welcome. Natalie said she felt she's been telling me that my problems are an acceptable part of being human. The problem was my image of what it was to be human. It was that half-born state—head out, being with God, seeing the world, body safe inside mother, not yet having to breathe.

My photography is from that place of being with God, head out in the world, eyes seeing, before body was born. Most of my pre-1976 photography was this. I sense my new photographing begins to be from a place of wholeness, in body, fully born, yet still with God.

April 22, 1981

My eyes have been hurting a lot the past few days. "I don't want to see." Wondering what scene I don't want to see, what early trauma. Then it changed to "No, it's not that I don't want to see; it's that I don't want to feel what I felt when light first hit my eyes."

Pain, terror, fear of being killed, body feeling raw, all the birth stuff at once. Cellular-level separation—intense grief and rage. Eyes open wide, mouth open, feeling "They've killed her, they've taken away everything that is good." Still crying as I write.

This level of fully re-experiencing birth was never reached while working with my eyes closed.

Another piece of the puzzle emerges. Again I feel amazement, awe and wonder.

For vaginal birth, the light comes after the hell part is over, at the moment of release. For caesarean-born people it accompanies both heaven and hell. I think I will do more eyes-open meditation.

May 2, 1981

Angie spoke of me, as caesarean, believing at a cellular level that I am separate. I realize I assume a judgment comes with this—that I am not supposed to feel separate, that I should feel connected. Well, I'm tired of faking this "relatedness," whatever that is supposed to be.

On the other hand, whenever I feel myself merging with someone, I get inner messages that it's not OK, that I should stay separate. Sexual taboos are part of this. Privacy stuff is, too.

The old "family" message is: I should be separate.

The new "transpersonal" message is: I should be connected.

Conflicting "shoulds."

Late spring through early fall 1981 was a busy time externally and internally. I went to New Hampshire to be with family while I worked on the caesarean birth slide-show I hoped to present at the Association for Transpersonal Psychology (ATP) conference. I felt I needed to return home to where this adventure started for me. Otherwise my work would be like the proverbial castle built on sand.

May 3, 1981

Yesterday I decided to go to New Hampshire. I already see how much tension I have beneath the delight of having decided to go. The decision to go came during internal work when I surrendered to cold, depression and willingness to die.

In last night's dream, I was in a class Angie was teaching. She handed out little folders and drawings she'd made for each of us. She handed me one with "Joint Jane" written on the cover. Inside was a picture of a two-headed me. Left half in a beautiful meadow, right half in a gloomy building full of blue-gray shapes. I asked if she would talk with me about sharing the caesarean birth stuff with Mother. She said, " Oh no, that is for you to work on alone." (*See Figure 12*)

Figure 12—Joint Jane

In preparing my slide show I did more drawings to illustrate some of the dreams I'd had during the preceeding few years. Among them was the 1973 dream that had started my inner journey. It had taken eight years of living with that dream to become objective enough to draw it. Even so, creating a visible image was very difficult. The dream still evoked many strong emotions and judgments. The eyes-open inner work I was beginning to do probably helped me to be willing to see the images manifested. Drawing them was part of my self-healing process. I share them here (See Figure 13, overleaf) in the hope that they will facilitate the self-healing journeys of other people.

Figure 13—Initiation Dream

Figure 13a—Victim

Figure 13b—Aggressor

Figure 13c—Alone

Figure 13d—Strangers

Figure 13e—Birthday Party

May 8, 1981

Meditation with eyes open. Eventually feeling a tremendous sense of loss, falling away from the pure light into the lesser light of earthly forms. Releasing some of the sadness and anger. Thinking of the experience (April 11, 1977) of falling into a well and the sliding-down-the-mountain dream (August 5, 1978). Both times I got scared and stopped before hitting the bottom. Allowing a little of the bottom to be experienced now. Absolute outer darkness for a moment. Then a few moments of an inner "light" within that darkness. So much of my photographing of nature was an attempt to reach back to that pure inner light.

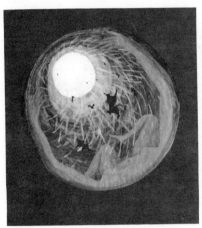 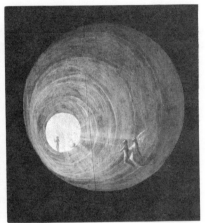

Figure 14a—Falling into Physical Form ("The Well" by Jane English)

Figure 14b—Floating out of Physical Form ("Ascent to the Empyrean" by Hieronymus Bosch)

At the Oakland Museum's Continuum show on life after death, I realized the after-death tunnel leading to light is the same tunnel I experienced falling into a well—falling away from the light in birth. The same sense of loss is described by people returning from near-death experiences. My painting looks similar to the one there. (*See Figure 14*)

May 9, 1981

Planning to spend time with a friend talking about caesarean birth. Feeling some tension. Realizing I will be opening deeply to her. Trusting her. Memories of similar openings with other people, all eventually followed by painful conflict, shutting down and separation. Fear of this happening again. Then a new understanding and a lot of emotion. In opening to each other, both of us will become aware of our birth-learning. Since our births were different, we won't necessarily agree with and support each other's birth-learned world-view. During this we may feel temporarily as if we are being attacked. But it is only our habits and illusions being questioned. Knowing this in advance, there is a chance we can maintain our friendship through such times of conflict.

Much crying as I realized this. I wish I had known it and been able to say it to past friends. Also the realization that, in therapy or school or at home, I often assume that any conflict is my problem and that the therapist or teacher or parent is more advanced than me. While this is true in some ways, my different birth-learning calls their birth-learning into question. So it's not all my problem.

I told my friend all this. I said I wanted her to be a friend and fellow traveller, and for us to dance together at a deep level and to accept and transmute whatever gets stirred up.

May 10, 1981   Meditation

Aware of a deep fear in relation to Mother. I've always felt wrong and guilty when I go out of her sphere mentally, emotionally and perceptually, as well as physically. When I surpass her. Though this has not been so strong a feeling since her spider-bite. Perhaps she has a "not having given birth" feeling that corresponds to my "unborn" feeling.

May 13, 1981   Bodywork

As she worked gently on my chest, all the work I've ever done on breathing flickered by. Tension in my face. Letting go and finding a big smile there. Thoroughly enjoying the help with breathing. After the huge defeat of allowing breathing to be started, I think I enjoyed being breathed by those big hands. Such luxury. Then as the body worker moved on, I felt angry at the help stopping. "I don't want to do it all by myself." Really pissed off. Somehow I never got that sense of freedom and connection with my own breathing. Alway associated it with someone helping me.

May 28, 1981   Dream

At Dick's house at Esalen. Feeling insecure and shy. Dick and his wife tell me to use an iron-lung respirator. They help me to get inside it. I feel such release as it breathes for me.

May 28, 1981   Bodywork session

Immediately open with the bodyworker. Told her the above dream. I sense she is teaching me new integrated body patterns. Love. Being properly mothered. Birth learning, but without the bad parts of labor.

June 1, 1981   Part of a dream

After a feast near an ancient ceremonial site, Stan says he is beginning to understand dependence better. This seems to be a result of my caesarean birth work. I feel we are equals.

June 4, 1981

Remembering Tom Ednie's comments on caesarean-born people not knowing the ethical stage in Kierkegaard's philosophy because it is rooted in the experience of labor. I feel a connection between this and the caesarean-born person's sense of no boundaries, of not knowing limits. Ethics are a code of limits. Since I, as a caesarean-born person, have no birth-learned feeling for these limits, I am often left with tension as I try to figure them out. I don't know quite what was expected of me and feel it is not OK that I don't know. One way of dealing with this is to get rigid and to stay far within the "acceptable limits," whose location I am unsure of. I think a lot of the unnamed fear I feel around family has to do with those limits.

I was increasingly interested in working more closely with Ralph Metzner. I felt that a way of transforming and transcending my birth learning would be to experience more fully some of the inner states he had described and given us tastes of in his classes and workshops I had attended from 1978-1981. These classes at California Institute of Integral Studies included light-fire meditation, androgyny, symbols of transformation, altered states of consciousness, alchemy and psychophysiology.

June 19, 1981   Dream

I am in a line of students waiting to consult with Ralph. He says we'll talk right now, even though a lot of students are waiting. He tells me I have great healing potential but that something keeps going wrong. I tell him the problem is related to my caesarean birth, especially to the relationship pattern of all-or-nothing. I say I am working on this. I feel a little surprised at how confidently I spoke. I start to leave, but he gets up and walks with me.

July 6, 1981

I talked with a non-labor caesarean-born woman. She affirmed the all-or-nothing relationship pattern and the tactile defensiveness that seem to be caesarean-born people's traits. She had a strong physical and emotional reaction to what I said. I could feel the intensity. What are my responsibilities when I abruptly stir up in others, awareness of caesarean birth patterns, an awareness that has emerged slowly for me? I pretty much ran away from her as gracefully as I could.

Talking to this woman activated in me a strong aversion to other caesarean-born people. Afraid of their dependence and needs, afraid I will push them away violently. Then thinking of caesarean-born people who have helped me with inner work, putting myself in their shoes in relation to me. Seeing how well they did, and feeling gratitude. I seem to be intending to hide behind my words and images and not deal with what they activate in people. Then I let go of the fears and accepted the possibility of doing awareness work with caesarean-born people. I actually like this idea. Image of collaborating with the people who helped me. Seeing myself as their friend and co-worker, as another person who has transformed the caesarean birth dynamic. I have transformed it with their help and thus have emerged with fewer scars. Such wonderful people they are.

I slept and awoke with a new sense of possibility about this project.

I presented my slide show at the ATP conference in the beginning of August. It was an initiation, a beginning of sharing my journey.

August 23, 1981

Last night I went to bed feeling negative. I knew I didn't want to go back to Mendocino, where a lot of my birth memory surfaced.

This morning I worked with this feeling by going through my caesarean birth slide-show in my mind, focusing on merging with the doctor, then being rejected. Still reacting emotionally to that part. Feeling as if I am in the hall with the closed doors. Stuck, depressed. Not knowing what opening the door to the unknown might be like. Not knowing how to do it. Thoughts of giving up and letting myself die.

Wondering how I will get through this when I show the slides to Ralph. Knowing this whole pattern in me gets activated with him. Imagining telling him that I hope the slides will get me into the merging, but that I'm unsure I can allow it, and if I do allow it, that I can resolve it differently. Then internally opening to him deeply, putting my life in his hands (the doctor's and/or Ralph's). Being breathed for.

All this so far is familiar from past explorations. Then something new emerged. A shadowy older female figure floated in from the left. The nurse watching me and the doctor. She took me when the doctor handed me away. Her heart wasn't open. She was businesslike. I merged with her and took on that pattern. Feeding schedule in the nursery, pain, closing down. Nothing I could do; at the mercy of the rigid structure. Without having experienced the limits of labor, the encounter with the nurse and nursery was one of my first encounters with limitation, and it should be seen as part of the birth. It is imprinted at that depth.

Feeling all this in body and emotions. Then sleep. Dream of having breathing tubes connected to a tank of water, which the air bubbles through. I could let go completely if I lay in the water and breathed through the tubes, but I fear the disapproval of some older women watching. I get into a smaller bathtub and let go somewhat. I keep myself covered with towels so they won't see me naked.

So good that all this keeps emerging. I see that often the emotions connected with what is not yet conscious (in this case, the nurse) get tangled up with what had previously emerged (merging with the doctor).

Chapter 5

Earth: Transformation and Healing

Having quite fully explored the fire, water and air elements of myself in relation to caesarean birth, I needed to give it external form, to connect with the element earth. The forms I worked on were a slide show and a book. When I asked Ralph Metzner to help me, he said the only way he would work with me on it was in therapy. The parts of me that still were attached to my caesarean birth-learned patterns were insulted. But a deeper part of me intuitively knew he had made a good choice, and in October 1981 I agreed to begin therapy.

Therapy was a commitment to a higher aspect of myself, to something deeper than all the birth learning. I revisited much of the inner territory I had journeyed through previously, and this time I had the tools to do a more systematic job of transforming what I met.

In retrospect, I see that before I could send this work out into the world in a way that would be helpful to others, I had to let go of my obsession with it. Paradoxically, that felt like failing, like giving up on communicating what I had learned. Only when I let go the physical, earth element of the caesarean birth patterns as they were manifest in the form and the tensions of my own body could I give this knowledge a new, external form. Those patterns now live mostly in the body of this book rather than in my body. It has been a death and a rebirth.

October 5, 1981

After giving my caesarean birth slide show, I talked with a psychiatrist friend about dependence and connectedness. I realized I have often misperceived inner connectedness. I called it clinging and judged it to be bad. In work with Ralph, I begin to allow the connectedness just to be.

October 25, 1981

Anger at Ralph's intervention in therapy. Not trusting him any more. The moment at which he seemed to impose his will on me felt like a time warp, a tunnel through time, touching on many similar situations. Then an implosion, all the "out there" becoming "in here." Feeling what I do in response to intervention: contract, shut down, a kind of suicide. A feeling of ugliness, of wanting to eliminate me from the world. Intense contracting. Hands over ears. Not wanting to hear. Curling as tight as possible. Breathing hard. Feeling myself forced open, uncurled, but now with awareness of doing it myself. Holding on to head hard for a long time. Image of Ralph being there. Wanting him to just observe me, to trust me. Slowly releasing. Images of birth, the unfolding.

November 2, 1981   Meditation

Awareness of identifying with silence and stillness! Perhaps an imprint or memory of the nursery. This manifests as a suppression of movement, especially holding breath.

November 13, 1981

Realization yesterday that I don't have to push through things and that I don't have to not push through things. Vaginal birth and caesarean birth patterns are both optional! They are both tools to use when appropriate.

November 19, 1981

Meditating on the thought of showing my slide show to myself. Wondering if I'd allow myself to get into it and not shut down. Then the idea of showing it in my mind's eye. Amazing experience! A quick run-through. Tag ends of visual, physical, mental and emotional stuff as I went through each stage. Some new heart openings in the birthday party. Joy and delight and appreciation for all my "dancing teachers," the people who labor with me and don't criticize my not knowing the vaginal birth dance. Such love and such playfulness.

November 21, 1981   Dream

I go into some hilly farm country with a farmer guide. Everywhere farmers on tractors are plowing fields. My guide takes me to his field. It is mostly plowed, except for an area on the far right side. In the unplowed area are dead stalks of last year's crops and a green squash vine. On it are several squashes in various stages of development. The farmer demonstrates how to graft them into another plant. He says the best way is to make a long, diagonal cut. He cuts off a young squash with a long cut that continues down into the body of the squash. He says it is important to do this so the squash and its new, more vertical stalk can make full, deep contact and merge and grow together.

Ralph said he'd dreamed of flying over vegetable gardens the same night. Says maybe he is my gardening consultant.

This dream goes way beyond caesarean birth, but seems to connect with it in the cutting and as a process that involves radical separation done to allow new growth and connections to form. Caesarean birth is a cosmic experiment.

November 29, 1981

Inner exploration. Much body awareness. Fantasy of being with Ralph. Less resistance to acknowledging the reality of the inner, of an invisible realm. Feeling safe. Allowing images of touch. Feeling rooted in him, cared for and nourished, not criticized or judged, very much accepted. Then dependency fear. Fear that he'll cut me off, get tired of me.

A memory of reading about tree-like existence in the womb. The baby, cord and placenta rooted in the uterus. This is what I was experiencing. The bonding with the doctor and the sudden separation from him after birth was a rerun of the uprooting and cutting off from Mother. Then I allow Ralph in the invisible realm to more fully enfold me. Not so much fear of being cut off. I don't have to do anything. This kind of inner connection is always available. Image of him giving birth to me. Different from the fantasy of being given birth that emerged after inner merging with Stan. That was strong, physical vaginal birth. With Ralph it is more subtle, and paradoxically, the "giving birth" seems to consist of becoming aware of inner connection. Then the outer separation seems easy and playful.

Back to sleep, more dreams: Beautiful birds, deer, chipmunk and a possum. Later, as I sat on the couch, I thought of the house being full of these wonderful animal spirits. I looked down and saw the cat, who had been asleep beside me, staring wide-eyed at me. He looked for a long time, then put his head down, still looking at me out of the corner of his eye.

Today's Tarot cards: Empress, Aeon, Hierophant. Earth mother and the two cards with father, mother, child. And the Aeon has the floating fetuses, too.

Once again, going deeply into birth material gave me access to a larger, transpersonal or spiritual reality. The dream, the apparent presence of animal spirits sensed by the cat and the synchronicity of the Tarot images with the earlier inner work are examples of what can be more easily experienced when one is open to this larger reality. Birth is a doorway between realms. It is guarded by demons who are one's repressed memories of birth.

December 29, 1981   Dream
I am in a flower garden outside the house I live in. I step carefully so I don't hurt the crocuses and pansies Mother planted. A lot of water is flowing into a hole under a cement block at the end of the row of flowers. I am afraid the flowers will be washed down the hole and am ready to uproot them to prevent this. A light is turned on down in the hole, and I see a work room with a tiled floor. Men, some black and some white, are dressed like butchers in white coats and caps, and they are carrying cleavers. I ask what they are doing in a room under the garden so near my house. They look at me and don't say anything. I see a woman with stiff bandages across her chest and around her throat. I get scared and run into my house, locking doors behind me. I know they can break the locks.

Later on in the dream I realize the woman in one of my projections; she reflects my throat and neck tensions. Then I am outside the house again and see some of the people down below. I also see some young children being squeezed up through a transparent plastic column. This has something to do with vaginal birth. Standing there I experience an orgasm. Awoke here. This is so similar to my August 11, 1977 dream of the baseball field.

This dream was a message that even though things appeared to be going well for me on the surface, I was running away from a deeper layer. I wanted the journey to be done all at once as in a caesarean birth. I didn't like going through the same material over and over. The dreams and therapy work in the next few entries are from a time of going through "old" material with new insights and more release. Someone once told me it takes a lifetime to come to terms with one's birth. Perhaps I need more patience.

January 2, 1982

Today I was in a hard, lonely, unnourished space. But I learned something important. The pain I fear in the future—physical, mental, emotional pain—is memory of past pain. Some of it is birth patterns. I begin to take care of myself now.

January 20, 1982   Dream

I am inviting people to a feast at Esalen. Dick comes toward me looking stormy and angry. I am open with him, not defensive. I take both his hands and look into his eyes. He relaxes some, but tells me I am to meet with him to talk some about negative things I have done. He pulls out a letter I had written to him. It is a warm letter, full of love. I can't see what he doesn't like. Then he points out a P.S. In it I comment that he is taking a long time to reply. It could be a neutral comment, but I can see it would be easy to take it as a criticism. I start to cry. I tell him that now I see I may have been negative.

Awoke here. An insight came immediately. I often express the positive and then immediately follow it with negative. That must hurt terribly coming into the openness created by my positive comments. I do this out of my fear that it isn't OK to be positive. I somehow expect a negative reaction to the very fact of my sending anything, positive or negative, toward people. I react with the caesarean birth pattern of defensiveness to anything coming toward me. I see now that I expect this same pattern in others, and that my own negativity following the positive actually creates this pattern. A self-fulfilling prophecy.

Again sadness and negative self-judgment at not knowing the vaginal birth dance, not knowing that contact is OK. I feel more ready to let go of the caesarean birth pattern. Interesting that Dick, another caesarean born, was in the dream. We are awful together when we both are defensive.

January 22, 1982

An insight in the middle of intense grasping, wanting and needing: I have gone into this contracted place over and over as a way of opening up and becoming receptive. By contracting to the point of exhaustion, I open. I also become open by being intruded upon. Such violent ways of opening. The caesarean birth pattern done over and over. So much pain. So much healing needed—and happening.

January 25, 1982   Bodywork

While she worked on my belly, I saw images of Mother's scar, images of pain. When I understood Mother chose it and experienced it willingly as part of caesarean birth, the pain became just intense sensation for me, then love. As a baby I didn't know the pain was being experienced willingly.

January 28, 1982

Subtle energy expanding out from heart center, hitting blocks, sweeping them away. When resisted, the energy created thoughts, emotions, images, as well as physical sensations and movement. The point of being in physical form seems to be to learn to resist in a coherent, elegant way, thus forming and manifesting the energy. Not to get rid of all the blocks, but to make them conscious and optional.

Breathing—image of a big hand on my chest. Fear of allowing complete exhalation, fear of being crushed. Body incoherent, easy movement and release in some parts, holding tension in others. Never whole release. A sense of something missing. Then seeing this perhaps as memory of vaginal birth from some other incarnation. Memory of the total letting go of birth. Both fearing and wanting that. Then some sense of being OK as I am in this incarnation without that experience. Seeing how I continually look for the total external containment and contact. Wanting it on the physical level. A thought that this time I'll get it from within, from the inner light of spirit! There is no vagina both big enough and wise and coherent enough to give me that on the physical level now, but the light of spirit always is big, wise and coherent.

February 2, 1982

Long, weird interior journey the last two hours. Doubting myself, Ralph and the usefulness of light-fire meditation. I got depressed, unable to see what good therapy is doing. Thinking Ralph offered me therapy with a negative, judging tone of voice. Then an explosion of anger as I throw off that negative I willingly took on. Imagine asking him if he loves me. Afraid his analytical mind will turn me into just another case, as with the doctor at birth.

I imagine asking him if it is OK if I die. I took his offer of therapy as a rescue. I find myself thinking the only way out of this dependence is to stop therapy or to ask it it's OK if I die.

For lifetimes I've been in situations where people are demanding that I die or demanding that I live. I've never made the choice or taken the responsibility. In living by other's demands that I live or die, I fell into a pattern of manipulation and trying to please. I see how I often misinterpret people, thinking that their liking me is a demand that I live.

February 12, 1982

Thinking about Ralph touching me in the last session. How much I wanted it and how scared I was of it. I tensed against his touch, pushing his hand away. I need to allow the same inner merging while he is touching me as I do without touch. And I need to learn to feel the inner connectedness after the touch is gone. I think I use sexual taboos to justify avoiding this contact and merging, to avoid the painful separation I fear might follow.

As I progressed in my inner journey, my outer journey with the caesarean material also progressed. At the urging of people who had seen my slide show, I wrote a brief article on caesarean birth and psychotherapy for the ATP newsletter. This was the first time I had sent my experience out into the world on its own.

March 21, 1982

Meditating. Waves of new sensation and opening in nose and face, alternating with old habitual tension patterns. Strong sensations in nose and sinuses. Felt like the beginnings of crying. Images of diving into water, swimming, nose clips, near-drowning. Allowing the sensation and the fear, with the knowledge I'm not drowning. Then to an even deeper level. Memory of air hitting these areas for the first time. Same intense sensations. Fear. This is what happens when newborns cry. I allow the sensation and fear, and I take several deep breaths. Tingling and light moving up into my head. Wonderful.

March 26, 1982

In the other morning's meditation, I felt creative, birth-giving energy moving out through my belly rather than downward. Fear of moving downward. Inner contact with all those beings whose heads were too big for vaginal birth and ended up being killed by craniotomies. In my bodywork session later, I learned to let energy and awareness flow into my legs. Good to have both patterns as options.

At the beginning of my journey I considered pictures I saw with my eyes closed to be imaginary, not real. And I considered thoughts and feelings I had about people who were not physically present to be fantasy.

Gradually, through a series of "coincidences," "synchronicities," and apparent extra-sensory perceptions, I have become sure that it makes more sense to act as if there is, behind, within and interpenetrating ordinary sensory reality, another invisible and equally real realm of being.

In these writings done while I was fumbling toward this concept, I variously refer to experiences from that realm as "on the inner," "in consciousness," "non-ordinary," "in the subtle or invisble realm," etc.

March 31, 1982

Deep inner journeying. Asking Ralph on the inner for a healing, even if it meant feeling as if he were killing me. Asked why do men kill women. Understanding their memory of feeling almost killed by the vagina at birth. I have the same feeling toward men. The experience of a man cutting my mother, pulling me out and squeezing me to get breathing going at my birth. I did more inner work with Ralph, unifying with him in consciousness and releasing mutual fear. Becoming a column of light.

April 10, 1982   Dream

I am at a transpersonal gathering. A woman healer is doing demonstrations. I volunteer. I'm a little uneasy. Don't want people to laugh at me. The healer gets inside a wooden box that has a hole for her head to stick out. I am to kneel on a step on one side of the box. She asks me what I am doing these days. As I start to tell her about the caesarean project, she waves an oversized baby bottle nipple in the air. I jokingly make sucking motions toward it. I start to say more about caesarean birth. She doesn't listen; instead, she shoves a black tube in my mouth. Before I can do anything, she turns on high pressure air that suddenly inflates a black balloon on the end of the tube. It bursts with a bang. Then a second one inflates and fills my mouth. I can't get it out. It seems to breathe for me. I fight it. Lots of sexual arousal. Lots of fear. I let go and pass out. She yells at me to come back, says I was going too far.

I woke up tense and scared.

In April 1982, I again moved, this time with a clear commitment to write a book on my experience of being born caesarean. I moved to a good "book-writing" environment that was secluded but still had access to the people and resources I needed.

May 3, 1982

Today I realized it's OK sometimes to want something.

May 6, 1982

Apprehensive about seeing Ralph tomorrow. Wanting him to hold me. Wanting to borrow his sense of wholeness while I see what I create for myself. Then, "I want you to hold me with your eyes." Many images of caesarean birth emerged. Meeting the doctor's eyes. Asking him in fantasy to hold me with his eyes while I learn to breathe on my own. I was androgynous then—sex unknown. Then being seen as female as he pulled me out. Taking on his attitude toward females. Body shouldn't be seen, etc. All this mixed with my later experiences with men. Imagining Ralph simply seeing me, both in ordinary reality and in the non-ordinary, inner realm. Giving me space to release the fear, shame and subtle tension with which head denies body.

May 8, 1982
One way to look at the present furor over the number of caesarean births being done is similar to the way I look at the nuclear question: Demons guarding a jewel. Caesarean birth is a powerful tool that is often misused. It is important to distinguish the tool from its uses.

May 13, 1982
To Ralph: You really trust I will comfortably move on to not needing your protected womb space any longer. I have never trusted I can do that. I have been afraid I will cling too long, then be rejected and torn away.

Concurrent with therapy, I began a series of rebirthing sessions. In them, one lies down for an hour or two and, with guidance from a trained rebirther, does connected breathing. Thoughts, emotions, images and patterns of tension in one's body surface into awareness and are released. This work complemented the therapy, allowing my body to participate more fully in the transformation I was experiencing. (See interview with Gayle Carlton in Part III for more on rebirthing.)

May 28, 1982
I ended my last rebirthing session aware of shutting down and defending against the professional attitude and dismissal I expected from the rebirther. Tonight I am aware that I create those attitudes. Taking back a projection. Wondering what the doctor felt when he handed me away. Tuning into his spirit, I felt his sadness and hurt. What a surprise! I've always thought I was the only one who was hurting in that moment. In meditation I helped him unify in consciousness with me and with all the other babies he delivered. Release of much sadness. With his scientific training he didn't know inner connection is possible, even when there is physical separation. Forgiving him for shutting down his heart and acting professional. It was his way of handling his own hurt. Much releasing in both my left and right sides. Then unifying in consciousness with Stan. Much of the same release and recognition, even more strongly felt.

How would an obstetrician with training in meditation handle a caesarean birth? What a question!

June 3, 1982
Up early after a late night. Feeling, "I don't want to get up, and I have to get up." Then it generalized to, "I don't want to be here, and I have to be

here," i.e. on earth, alive. That seems like the rock-bottom impasse and the source of the melodrama.

Seeing all this I feel a tiny bit better. Body says I don't want to; head says I have to. The healing begins.

Later—part of the great game seems to be to find out how separate we can pretend to be and still survive—personally, as a species and as a planet. We seem to delight in separating and unifying, in forgetting and remembering, in getting lost and finding ourselves.

June 6, 1982   Dream after showing my caesarean birth slide show

I am at a gathering of people. A healing process is being demonstrated. The patient gets into a large pillow. A second person pushed the pillow under water, then pulls it out and manipulates it forcefully with his hands and with another pillow. The person inside almost drowns and has to surrender totally to what is happening to his body.

As usual, birth stuff is activated in me by showing the caesarean birth slides.

June 14, 1982

Good rebirthing today. One big release came when images of shiny metal became connected with a lot of fear and yuck in body. Caesarean birth! In avoiding the feelings, I have been hanging onto the image.

During the summer of 1982, I began collecting the thoughts and experiences of caesarean-born people and others. These conversations were delightful. I was with fellow travellers and allies and no longer felt so alone on my journey. Records of these conversations are in Part III.

July 13, 1982

Lots of energy hitting a stuck place in my head. Wanting something. Opened to Ralph on the inner. Immediate relief, easing throughout the body. Didn't judge the contact. Didn't reach out for anything in particular from Ralph. Just opened.

This experience feels like a gift of grace. Perhaps the opening is what is important, not the opening *to* any particular person.

July 23, 1982

Difficult night. Life vs. death. Wanting Ralph to tell me it is OK to die. Physical memory of "must live." Finally an insight that eased things. The decision to be here is a moment to moment one. Not a "once and for all" thing that traps me here. Slept again. Woke with a healing song.

July 27, 1982

Hard session with chiropractor. I followed Ralph's suggestion of letting my inner physician unify with her inner physician. But I was too open on the personality level. I didn't know how to say no creatively. The spinal manipulation left me in pain and feeling scared. As at birth: surrendering my body, then being hurt. Maybe I need to learn a different kind of openness.

July 29, 1982

Another session with the chiropractor today. More fear of being hurt. I realized that the fear was connected with my expectation of being hurt. The I unified an inner healer I trust. Maybe what happened two days ago was my unifying with a distortion of the physician within, one that does invade, intrude and hurt. I told the chiropractor I needed her to go slower. She didn't force an adjustment even though a vertebra was out. I let go of the part of me that wanted her to push. Afterward I did more inner work, releasing my birth-learned image of the healer as one who hurts me. Carrying that image around, no wonder I've been scared of healers and healing.

Communicating what I was learning continued in the summer of 1982. I presented an up-dated version of the slide show twice more. At Rebirth International's annual Jubilee and again at the ATP annual conference. Both times there was a good two-way sharing of ideas and experiences.

September 3, 1982

Mothers trust their babies will initiate the birth process. The timing is the only unknown. I wasn't given that trust. I have been looking for it. In most births those present also trust the baby will initiate breathing. I wasn't given that trust either. I understood this after wanting Ralph to trust me to go way in to a deep place inside that is beyond words and time.

September 4, 1982

Tense. I fear my book won't be well received. I'm afraid people will think my images of caesarean birth are too violent. Afraid people will shut down because of the violence. Explored this fear and came to the birth itself. All those tense, shut-down people at my birth. I took on the fear and tension and assumed I was to blame, that I'd done something wrong. I think of the "This is caesarean birth" dream of a few years ago. The scared, tense people were there in the dream.

Why were they so scared? Tuned in to them and began forgiving and releasing. All I wanted was for someone to greet me. Someone open and not afraid. I was merging with everything around, so I took on their fears.

In a vaginal birth, the mother is there, and is open. She has to be in order for the birth to happen, although with drugs and forceps she can hold onto her fears and tensions. I have been looking for someone who can be with me exactly as I am. Someone to help me find that acceptance in myself. I think of being told a few years ago, "You will be beautiful when you find someone who doesn't want anything from you."

This exploration of caesarean birth again sheds light on some of the subtleties of the mother's role in vaginal birth.

September 7, 1982

Today's chiropractic work opened something. Just now I experienced feeling lifted up and out with love! That's how I go to a new level. One of the treasures of a caesarean birth.

September 9, 1982

After yesterday's emotional explosion, I thought of my friend's question. He asked if I am ready to learn to shut out other people's emotions, ready to have boundaries. Today after work with my chiropractor, what surfaced was sadness, love and forgiveness. Forgiving myself for taking on a lot of negativity. I didn't know about creating boundaries. And only now do I know that I didn't know.

September 13, 1982   Rebirthing

Breathed through a lot of fear. Then wondered if it was OK to stop for today. Insight that the baby not only initiates labor as a whole, but each contraction and the end of each contraction. I'd been carrying the message that it's not OK to end something until it is totally done. The pattern of caesarean birth—total and all at once. Now I see I can create the timing of the completion and of the temporary, partial completion at the end of each step. Probably the mother/child organism does it as a whole in labor, but from the child's point of view, he or she does it. Sadness from the times I had judged partial completion not OK and had invalidated what I had accomplished. Forgiving myself now for not knowing any better.

The next big insight was knowing that the caesarean birth pattern is the ability to take huge leaps, *with the help of others*. New Age group consciousness! Lots of light and love flowing through with this awareness.

The fear of being intruded on that I felt before doing this rebirthing here at home is itself part of the birth pattern. I was "safe at home" minding my own business when all hell broke loose at birth. So "safe at home" doesn't feel all that safe to me. Again part of the context becomes content.

September 22, 1982   Rebirth with Gayle

Talked for an hour about both being caesarean. Lots of mutual support. Much less fear of being intruded upon than when I work with vaginally-born people. Also aware we can create stuckness in mutual caesarean birth "blind spots." But vaginally-born people facilitate each others' inner journeys, so why not caesarean born-people?

She gave me time to let breathing flounder around before getting into a rhythm. So often I'd forced myself to breathe regularly and created fear and resistance. Sense of external demands as to how I breathe. Then some good work with touch defensiveness. I'd felt something soft missing around my face. She touched me gently, and I was afraid. Much appreciation of her knowledge of caesarean birth patterns.

September 29, 1982   After the home-birth of a friend's son

A few days ago, I had a semi-dream experience of my head jamming against something. Fear and shaking. Couldn't figure it out in terms of my birth and decided I must be tuning in to others' vaginal birth memories. Then I remembered a psychic's trance comment a few years ago that I'd complete the release of my caesarean birth patterns by experiencing my mother's birth. I also remembered a story of a person reliving caesarean birth, then going right on into a vaginal birth experience. It makes sense to consider the possibility of having a cellular memory of my mother's birth. My cells were formed in the context of her.

September 30, 1982

This morning I processed a lot of fear. It released in yet again opening to Ralph and allowing feelings of dependence and fears of rejection. Then I understood I was again being lifted up with love as we began work on a new aspect of the light-fire meditation. I saw that I'd been unaware that after I am lifted out with love, I integrate the change and make it my own. This awareness came from feeling that Ralph is giving birth to me, healing me, helping me reconnect with myself at a higher level. It also came from his comments on how one integrates these light tools, makes them one's own, rather than something taught by someone else.

So my way of changing is to be open, merged, dependent, lifted up with love, and then experience a time of integrating. So good to get this perspective. Now perhaps I can change without so much fear. Hidden by the fear of rejection was my need for separateness, integration and making the experience my own.

October 2, 1982

Worked with Ralph yesterday. I felt he was teaching me to heal myself. I saw that before the higher can lift me, it has to come down in! Intrusion and opening precede the being lifted up with love. I released from my heart a big chunk of birth-related fear that I had projected onto Ralph. Awoke happy today for the first time in a while.

October 27, 1982

I feel I should become exactly what people want me to be. This is part of why I push people away. I don't want to be this flexible, to surrender this much to outside forms. I feel I can be myself when I'm alone. Does this relate to not having gone down the birth canal? Not experiencing surrender to outside pressures on the physical level followed by the discovery that I survived them.

October 31, 1982

Lying in bed wanting to be touched and helped. Fantasy of having a child with Ralph. Then, "What if it has to be caesarean?" At a deep level I seem to assume it will be caesarean. Opening and release in belly. Seeing how much I'd been blocking the possibility of being operated on and of mothering a caesarean-born child. Seeing it was OK to go into the "taboo" fantasy of sex, child and family with Ralph. It was a doorway to an important piece of caesarean-birth work. Children come in relation to a man. To get in touch with my feelings about having a caesarean-born child, I had to fantasize about unifying sexually with a man I love. Much of my awkwardness with him was a deeper fear of being cut open in a caesarean operation.

December 3, 1982   Dream

I am in a clinic. Someone demonstrates the apparatus for using ether. I ask to smell it. I take a tiny whiff, then several deeper ones. I begin to feel uncoordinated, and I knock over the bottle of ether. Nurses rush to clean it up. I get another big dose and go off by myself. I lie down, curl and surrender to what is happening. Two nurses ask how I am. I don't want to talk. I just want them to hold me. I feel not OK with this. Feel they want me to talk, which I can't do without tensing up.

January 5, 1983

I habitually open totally to men, whatever energy they have. At some level I am totally vulnerable to negativity, even when I appear to resist it. Then an amazing connection—at birth, I had to open totally to the man who was hurting me in order to survive. Way in deep, I am still doing this. A deep fear of death driving that habitual openness and helplessness. Lots of energy release and relief in seeing this.

January 12, 1983   Dream

I have an electric candle with an amber colored bulb. Ralph takes a lighted match and touches it to the top of my candle's light bulb. The tip of the bulb melts, and it becomes an ordinary candle with a flame that reaches out beyond the glass. I awoke here Not nearly so scrunched as the past few mornings.

I like this dream. Electric lights glow because of electricity coming in on wires from somewhere else. A candle burns on its own! Being touched with his light tool (the match), I find my own inner light. I am no longer so dependent.

January 16, 1983   Session with Ralph

Letting myself sink in deep, entering stillness. Then Ralph asked what I was experiencing. I felt angry at the intrusion. Looking back, I can see this is also birth stuff. As I was sinking into the anesthesia, I was intruded upon.

I got scared I was sinking in too far. I asked Ralph if the fear was his or mine. He said it was mine. This is the first time I have had the presence to ask that question. I always assumed the fear came from the other person. It did at birth and at the near-drowning.

His acceptance of the fear allowed me to accept it. The fear went away, and I talked more with him about staying in contact. He reached in to me in a loving, matter-of-fact way. At birth and in the near-drowning I was rescued by fearful or angry people. My experience today is still a rescue, but I prefer a loving rescuer to a fearful one. Looking back at the "intrusion," I see it was perfectly timed. It gave me a chance to transform some of my fear and anger about intrusion, rescue, and help. Help is OK if it doesn't have emotional baggage along with it. I have often rejected help because I didn't want the baggage.

January 17, 1983

In caesarean birth one goes through an amazing change. One has to be open and accept the help of a group of people. Maybe my way has been to hold on and hold on until I had all my resources mobilized. Then open up, let go and fly, and know I have what I need.

January 18, 1983

I have been experiencing simultaneously a completion of my physical birth and a rebirth into a higher level of consciousness. I wonder if they go on simultaneously for people who are not non-labor caesareans. Even though we non-labor caesareans have easy contact with the light of spirit we don't know to share it because we aren't completely here yet. So we have to do this contradictory thing of first seeming to go away from the light toward the earth. At the moment we let go the the light and fully accept incarnation we discover we really have both—body and spirit.

January 22, 1983

All those people who were afraid I would die at birth, near-drowning and other times, also loved me. I threw out the love with the fear.

January 25, 1983

Sensation of big hands on my chest and back squeezing me. Image of energy going through body, image of orgasmic release. I did a little connected breathing (as in rebirthing). I felt anger; maybe the doctor's squeezing hurt, and I contracted and became angry. Then I felt a strong sense of not wanting to breathe, but I followed Gayle's suggestion from my last rebirthing and kept on breathing through that feeling. Then an insight, "I started breathing because I felt his (the doctor's) love, and I loved him. I wanted to be there with him and not go away into the blackness." Then anger came up at being left alone. "I started breathing, and then he left me there alone. He tricked me!" At that time I had interpreted the physical separation as also being inner separation.

This is the first time I have come to awareness of the moment when I actually chose to breathe, not out of fear, but out of love.

January 25, 1983

I was thinking about fantasy. My wondering if I am "making it all up" is a leftover from being told my inner world is fantasy. When I meet Ralph on the inner, it is not like an outer meeting, though I sometimes use images of the outer to help bring the inner into awareness. There is no separate being I meet. We become one, or maybe like cells in the same organism, following the organizing field. That's the real root of world peace. We all act in harmony, not as separate beings trying to harmonize, but from already being one. Separateness is cancerous when it is overdone. But separateness is not all bad. The earth experience is an adventure in separateness, in individuality. The trick is to be both at once, separate and unified.

January 27, 1983

In doing this caesarean-birth work, it is important for me to remember I am still in the process of transformation. I still carry both darkness and light. It is important to speak from my heart. When I do that, it is OK to speak of the darkness.

February 5, 1983

I did an inner journey. I set my timer for twenty minutes. At one point I began to worry about not having enough time to complete the journey. I realized that I should trust the timing would be perfect. It was.

When I worry that something will come too soon, I shut down and resist the flow of life and change. Then I do indeed experience change as being intrusive. When I trust, all goes well. There is flow.

This is the transformation of that terrible pattern: "It's too soon. I'm not ready, I don't want to be here." There was nothing wrong with the birth itself. The problem is the not trusting that the universe is perfect, not seeing that I am getting exactly what I need and that it is being given with love.

February 12, 1983   Dream

I sit at the corner of a newly plowed rectangular field that is mine. Ralph is planting plants around its boundary. They are like strawberry plants; they have runners that connect one plant to the next.

This dream is about boundaries, one of the big caesarean birth issues. And these boundaries are alive! They grow and change and are flexible. My image of boundaries has been one of static, rigid, non-living absolutes. This new image is wonderful.

Later, in a session with him, Ralph asked if it was he or I who was planting. I said he was and I was directing him. He asked me to continue the dream. I experienced him planting the rest of the plants. As he brought the runner from the last one to the first one, I reached out and we made the final connection together.

February 15, 1983

Thinking about completion of therapy with Ralph. Completion is wholeness is healing, a letting go of incompleteness, of separateness. On the way to the place deep inside where I find healing, I often go through a little of what it feels like dying. I usually am afraid of letting go to this in the presence of anyone, afraid they will become impatient with me. I think they too have to give up, give up on helping me. Perhaps in birth I began to breathe when the doctor gave up on my every breathing and was just there with me. To me that felt like love, and I felt attracted to it. Wow! I chose a world where I was accepted exactly as I am, where there were no demands on me. That is the moment I chose to breathe.

March 5, 1983

I remember a friend telling me that caesarean people feel pressure and don't know they can push through. His implication is that they can push through. But in birth they couldn't. After I grew past a certain point, my head wouldn't fit through the pelvic opening. Instead of pushing, I trust someone will reach in and lift me out.

With each of my therapists, I have had a lot of fear and resentment; I wanted something but didn't know then what it was. I wanted them to lift me out, to give birth to me. I became fearful and resentful. I thought I should do things all by myself, but didn't believe I could.

Ralph and I went through that place successfully a couple of weeks ago when he asked me who was doing the planting, and I said he was. He accepted that, and I was glad he did. I think he could feel it was true for me, and he respected that. We would have come into conflict if he had stayed with vaginal birth learning and said I had to do it myself.

I have been so hard on myself for not going the way people expect me to go, for not pushing through, for wanting so much help, for being dependent. Part of the cosmic agreement I had with my birth helpers was that they would help me come out, because I wouldn't be able to make it on my own.

My mother didn't know far ahead of time that my older brother would be caesarean. All during pregnancy she thought she'd have to labor with him. But with me she knew there would be no labor. She knew someone would lift me out. Her attitude during the pregnancy must have been quite different. Maybe I tuned in to it.

I want to learn about pushing through, but it has to be without the vaginally born persons' belief that if they *don't* push through they will die. For me it is just the opposite. I fear that if I *do* push I might die. So vaginally-born people can help me learn about pushing through, and I can help them learn about trusting that help will be there. Sometimes pushing is good, and sometimes trusting is good.

March 24, 1983

So often I have an impulse to sink way in deep. It seems like going into total inaction. But that is how I was born, the anesthesia. Somehow I believe real change has to be preceeded by fogging out. Sometimes when I want to do something, I seem to go into inaction. When I fully sink way in and feel the possibility of never doing anything again, new inspirations come to me. But most often I resist both the action and the sinking in, and I stay stuck in the middle.

April 1, 1983

Last night I was in darkness again. Wanting to die, not liking this painful experience of being in a body. Memory of all the times I haven't known what I wanted. All the fear and resentment at not getting my needs filled, the times of appearing manipulative.

Then I heard myself say, "I want you to show me what I need to do in order to survive." Memory of being shown how to breathe, and of being taught other things as a child. So often the teaching was accompanied by fear that I wouldn't survive. Ralph is offering me inner tools for survival without the fear. I don't have to constantly re-create the fear that surrounded birth.

I told Ralph about this and he said fear is appropriate and useful sometimes. What I don't need is constant fear.

Again I see that "progress" on this inner journey doesn't mean never again experiencing these dives into darkness. progress is knowing how to get through these times quickly and to bring back jewels of truth from those dark places.

The temptation is to create a nice, neat conclusion to the story of my journey. But grand conclusions don't fit my intention for this to be a rough, preliminary map. It is a set of footprints or steppingstones that will be useful to other explorers of the inner worlds, to caesarean-born people and to their friends, families and therapists.

I hope you will use the parts of my trail that feel right for your own journey and let the rest be. Follow other trails or strike off on your own and create a new path. May your journey be a good one!

I, too, am still journeying. But for now, my trail will not be marked with words.

A Note About the Journey:

In looking back over the material in Part II, I noticed a series of dreams that were maps, overviews, guides. All of them move from darkness to light, negative to positive, constriction to opening. Going back and re-reading just these dreams gives a good overview of the whole journey.

Date	Chapter	Dream Content
1973	1	Rape, murder, hallway, strangers, birthday
January 16, 1975	2	Keystone Park
January 26, 1975	2	Tree/hill/swamp/windows storms/sun
February 4, 1975	2	With Dick on a new path
April 17, 1978	3	Astronaut
July 27, 1979	4	"This is caesarean birth", Sungod
March 9, 1981	4	Joint Jane
June 19, 1981	4	Appointment to work with Ralph
November 21, 1981	5	Farmer, squash plant
January 12, 1983	5	Electric candle
February 12, 1983	5	Strawberry plant boundaries

Part III

Fellow Travelers

I think of us as explorers, pilgrims, or wanderers spending evenings sitting by the fire, each one telling tales of their adventures and explorations. We learn from each other and together create maps of new territory.

Conversation with Marilee James King (*caesarean-born therapist*)
June 28, 1982

Marilee James King is a psychotherapist with a transpersonal orientation. At present, she lives in the San Francisco Bay Area.

Marilee was the first other non-labor caesarean to see my slide show. Her strong positive response greatly encouraged me to continue the work that has ultimately led to this book.

M: I had felt for a long time in my life that certain things wouldn't work for caesareans. When I saw the slide show for the first time, I was profoundly moved because it was a validation of that feeling, In your slide show, whenever there were walls, it struck something deep in me. I think it has to do with not knowing how to break through a wall. Before I saw the slide show, I knew there might be lots of differences, but I didn't have any actual theory. One of your drawings that resonates with me is the drawing where people are bringing you gifts. That's what I am still in the process of learning. My experience of others has to do with merging and learning from them, in that way receiving gifts I didn't have when I started.

J: One of the things I think about when I look at that picture (of the birthday party in the 1973 dream, *See Figure 13*) is that those are all the people who have been willing to labor with me. Giving me the gifts of some identity, of boundaries. They were giving me some sense of myself.

M: I might not use the same words, but the process is the same. Something about people willing to labor with me is significant to my own process.

J: What is the quality of a situation where somebody is laboring with you?

M: Willing to go through a tangle with me and to come out the other side with an understanding. I know a lot of people in superficial ways, and then we have to cross a bridge together to get to something deeper. Going across the bridge is a struggle. If I don't cross that bridge with them, there's never a bonding. There has to be a willingness on their part to struggle with me.

J: The people who are willing to labor with me are the ones who are willing to set aside all their preconceptions of what is going on.

M: Because what is going on is somehow directed by a higher wisdom. Two people are getting in there and discovering the process between them. That's my experience of it. Then they emerge on the other side where the process is understood intuitively. Not that anything specific or concrete has worked out. The process has a different shape with every person, but there's this process that has to happen for a connection to form. If a person I am moving toward a deeper relationship with is not willing to grapple with our energies, the relationship never happens. We just get to that phase and then have to pull back over and over again. When

I encounter that struggle, I find myself asking, "Am I willing to go through this?" I find it is quite a strain on me, probably because some of the birth pattern is occurring there.

J: You have to give up another little piece with this person.

M: I am confronting my whole birth process in order to bond with someone.

J: And you are confronting the other person with theirs. If they're not ready to do that, then you can't meet at that deeper level. You can be sociable with each other, but you can't really unify.

M: My belief is that there are at least two types of caesareans: the mobilizer and the rescuee or victim. I am a mobilizer. When I have a task to accomplish, I mobilize the resources I need. There's a fine line between mobilizing what you need and being rescued. The rescuee turns to everyone and says, "Help me." Mobilizers also say, "Help me," but they muster up for themselves the resources they need. I may not look like I am mobilizing; it often appears to be giving up.

J: In what way?

M: It's like being in the womb and knowing I will be rescued. "Now pick me up. Now make me breathe," etc., rather than feeling, "Oh no, what's happening to me?" Relaxing into the support rather than being saved. It is a gift, this ability to mobilize and this knowledge that the universe is supportive. You never had to go down the birth canal alone; you were just lifted out.

But the paradox is that while we have this great transpersonal knowing at the core of our being, we also have to function in the ordinary world. The problem is in dealing in the ordinary while still remembering that knowing. It's easy to forget it, to lose the sense of, "Look at all I am able to do" and fall into , "Oh, will I ever get through this?" I get caught in feeling like I don't know how to do this on my own, rather than trusting that help will be there.

J: How do you see the patterns of your birth manifested in your thoughts, emotions, ways you perceive the world, and ways you behave or hold your body? What are the resonances between things you experienced in your birth and patterns later on?

M: What's difficult for me is the process. There is an incredible knowing of possibility and of the highest, in groups, friendships, in love affairs, whatever. I can almost always see the "We are one" of the situation. I'll hold the vision, and it'll be an amazing vision. But the getting from here to there is where I get stuck.

J: What happens?

M: I get misunderstood as I try to explain and share my vision with other people.

J: Be as specific as possible. Having danced the same dance, I understand it, but I think the specifics will help others.

M: When I was doing a counseling internship, I had the vision that the group of interns had reached the level where we could become a real counseling center. Each person would move from student to professional and get paid. I saw it as not very hard to do and saw exactly how to do it, knowing that each person in the group fit in it perfectly. When I communicated the idea, the response was somewhat skeptical, but pretty good.

But as we tried to get from where we were as interns to being professionals, things got impossible, and I had no vision for getting through it. We got bogged down in things that, to me, seemed insignificant and not at all heading toward the vision. We were working, not on the vision, but on the process to get there. I wanted to be there already. I withdrew from the group. I went back at one point and said, "Look, why don't we all just jump levels and be there and encompass this?" That outraged everyone. They said, "How can you come in here and say we'll just jump levels?"

J: This fits in with one of the ways I have conceptualized the difference between the vaginally-born dance and the caesarean dance. In the vaginally-born dance, things move and change like labor, in waves, going out and coming back, expanding and contracting; it's a struggle, slow moving, difficult. And the caesarean process is direct, total, and intense, like an arrow, uni-directional. That's what you were describing. You wanted to do it totally and all at once. You knew this was possible because you had done it in birth. They all wanted to labor.

M: They wanted to think there was a long process between where they were and where they wanted to be.

J: How can you deal with that kind of situation?

M: I haven't discovered that yet. What happens for me is that things move too slowly, and my first response is to go where things can happen faster. My second response is to start examining what is going on in me. I want to learn to put out my ideas without so much attachment to them.

J: Are there any other resonances of birth you see in your life?

M: I hate limits on myself. I once described humans as being limitless. The person I was talking to looked at me in horror. But there is a feeling in me that I am limitless in the sense of being of the universe; I am a cosmic being. I was raised a strict Catholic, but my own inner learning was a much more compassionate understanding of being connected, rather that the dogma that I was given. I don't have an easy time with boundaries of any kind. I don't like time limits. I like to feel that my time is open. I connect to the birthday party picture in your slide show where the man has the round hoop in his hand.

J: He is also caesarean. The important part of the hoop is that it symbolized to me the open space he gave me in therapy. But you can't recognize the space without the boundary, the ring. I am beginning to appreciate boundaries.

M: I don't know where my own boundaries are. That's why the intimate space is so important to me. There's not a lot of boundary there. The person I am intimate with is able to come right in. With a vaginally-born person, there are layers and layers of boundaries. In a group, people come in, and I don't realize I have let them in psychically and emotionally as deeply as I have.

J: You take on group energy?

M: Absolutely. A vaginally-born would have a definite limit that you would sense and not push beyond. I'm not sure I put up limits clearly.

J: I have the same feeling. It's as if it's not OK to say no.

M: Yeah. There's something about going down the canal that maybe says, "Yes, no, yes, no." The pushing, the moving, the contractions.

I want to tell you about a guided imagery experience. It is really significant. I did it with someone I had "gone across the bridge with" and felt understood by. He first led me through a relaxation of my body, then took me on a journey with guided imagery. We started out in a field, and he took me from the field to a stream, finding a way to get down the stream. Then I was in this ocean, and I kept running into little parts of myself. Then he brought me down even deeper and had me find a trap-door at the bottom of the sea, and I opened it and went down into that. So I would say I was pretty far regressed at that point.

I went into a cave, and I walked to the end and there was a wall. I could tell he wanted me to break through the wall. I felt I was disappointing him because I couldn't figure out how to get through the wall. I felt stuck. So he pulled back and didn't force me. I went around the wall and down into another chamber below the wall. There was a bronze stage there, and I was on the stage. I liked it for a while, but I was uncomfortable being alone. So after entertaining the audience, I brought them up on the stage and formed a big circle. I led them through a wonderful exercise where we related as beings with equality.

Then I went back to the outside of the wall. The man who was guiding me asked if I could get through it. I said no, but that I'd go down and get all those people. I brought them up to the inside of the wall, and I gave them tools. I went back around the wall and directed them. I'd tell them to work a little further over, to keep coming, etc. They broke through the wall, and some water was able to flow. Then I came back up the way I came in. I didn't get congratulated. I didn't need anything from the people. It happened, it was done, and now it was time for me to move on. That's mobilizing.

I sensed from working with this therapist that he was disappointed I hadn't broken through. I felt he thought this was a place that I needed to grow in. When I saw your slide show, I was amazed. The guided imagery experience of mine was my birth pattern.

J: Pushing through was an issue for me in rebirthing; I had a sense of "I can't push through." My rebirther helped me to push through with my own breath. She was the first person to offer me the possibility of pushing through without herself being emotionally attached to my doing it.

M: When it's offered as a gift, it's one thing. When it's a should, it's another.

J: Someone who has transcended his or her own birth pattern can offer it to you as a possibility. We too have to learn to offer our birth pattern as a gift, rather than saying, "You *should* be able to get from here to there without any struggle or process."

What suggestions do you have for caesarean-born people who want to know what role their birth plays in their lives? How do you explore the territory? I ask this of you in your role as a therapist.

M: First is to recognize that birth pattern plays an important part in their lives. Your slide show was significant to me because it was the first time I had heard anyone say anything in public about caesarean birth. Another suggestion is to find other caesarean-born people and to discover commonalities. Also, talk to their mothers about their births.

J: What suggestions would you give vaginally-born parents who are to have a caesarean-born child, in terms of preparing themselves for birth?

M: The parents could get in touch with their own birth patterns. Inner work on themselves would be significant. Also examine any feelings they have about caesarean birth, to work through anything negative. Let go of any judgment on caesareans and see it as a different way of being. I hope this book will make people understand that we are one *and* we are different. To get in touch with the positive parts of caesarean birth and to make it as trauma-less as possible.

J: Do you have any specific suggestions?

M: I suggest all sorts of soft things, warm water to bathe the baby in as it's born, soft lighting, having the father in the room, using a regional anesthetic. Make the birth as conscious as possible. It's a child coming in, a new beginning, a new way of being. The child is born without a sense of struggle. The parents should look at how it will be when they run up against their own belief that you have to struggle, and the child doesn't share it with them. Spend some time talking to caesarean-born people. Talk with parents of other caesarean-born children about the differences. I believe that massage can help caesarean-born children learn about their boundaries.

J: It's clear that some good things happen in labor. Stimulating the respiratory system, getting fluids out of the lungs, integrating the nervous system, giving a whole body experience, a sense of limits and boundaries. What should a parent do for a caesarean-born child who hasn't been labored with?

M: Teach him or her what process is about, how to get from that place to this place and what amount of struggle is involved. At the same time, the parents can allow the child to teach them that ability to know the limitlessness, the transpersonal.

Reinforce the idea that the caesarean was something acceptable, rather than, "Poor you, you had a caesarean birth." There may be an odd feeling as the child starts to relate to other children. The parents can help by reassuring the child, "Part of this is because you have a different birth pattern." The other thing would be to encourage the child's understanding of the vaginal birth pattern.

J: You were talking about teaching children that they were born by a different process. It seems to me there is a fine line between appreciating the difference and using the differences as an excuse for all kinds of behavior.

M: We are talking about conscious parenting where the parents look at what gifts a caesarean child might have and what a caesarean child might need.

J: It's only been a hundred years that there have been many caesareans.

M: It's something that needs to be looked at. Perhaps it's a new energy that beings are bringing into the world. It's happening with the larger number of caesareans. My mother told me as a child that everybody who was anybody had their children that way! That "better than you" stuff only worked partially. Already I was so different that the "better than" was not good. I'd prefer "different" to "better than." This has to do, for me, with the whole transition that our planet is in. Going from an ego-centered view of the world to one that is more inclusive, that sees differences as gifts, without judgments on them. Working with a synergistic model.

J: The phrase "appreciation of differences" was given to me a few years ago, and it has been a real help.

M: How accurate can astrological things be for caesareans?

J: I feel that it is accurate, but at another level. In vaginal birth the time of the birth is partly the baby's choice because chemical changes in the baby initiate labor. I see that choice being made by a caesarean at a high level, a transpersonal level. At an ordinary level, you'd say a caesarean didn't choose the time of birth.

What thoughts do you have on all of this for psychology, education, transpersonal and spiritual theory and practice, for the evolution of consciousness, for conscious evolution and for other areas? What are the broader implications?

M: The implications have to do with the idea of differences. My experience of spiritual work comes from a place of, "We are one, let's learn from each other." Your birthday party in other words. I'm bringing my dish, everybody is bringing theirs, and we are all going to have something together. We are discovering our oneness, and at the same time we are becoming aware of our differences. That's what caesarean-born people can bring to the planet. We've got a different order with us, and we live in a place where there is an established order. Yet we see the struggle that's going on in things such as the feminist movement and minority movements. All these people are saying we're not worse, we're different. That's what we're saying also. We're bringing it from a place as basic as the birth pattern.

Conversation with Natalie Ednie   *July 1, 1982*

Natalie Ednie is the mother of seven children, all born in natural, undrugged vaginal deliveries. She is the wife of Tom Ednie, M.D., has studied Gestalt with Fritz Perls, and Sensory Awareness with Charlotte Selver and is a long-time student and admirer of Tai Chi and Taoism.

Natalie was a fellow student with me in the sensory awareness study group in 1975-76. She held my hand (sometimes literally) through the most emotionally chaotic part of my journey. She had a way of providing enough support that I could continue my explorations without so much help that I would lose my desire to find a way out of inner knots.

J: You've labored with seven children, so you have lots of experience with labor.
N: I'm an expert!
J: What do you see as some of the most significant aspects of labor in terms of what it gave to your children physically, psychologically and spiritually.
N: One thing jumps out right away. During the labors I've had, which have been natural labors, I always had the sense I was giving my children the best possible start. I had absolute faith and trust in the process of labor even with my first born. I felt strongly that nothing ought to interfere. It was somehow important for the child. I didn't understand that it was important for me, too, until afterwards.

There's nothing like laboring with a baby to let you know that it is yours, that it's part of you, that it came from you. All of that is indelibly imprinted with the labor. I used to see caesarean women walking around the hospital looking a little bit distant. They looked through the nursery window without that passionate attachment that I felt. Of course, they were envied because they weren't sore.

J: They were just as sore in a different place.

N: Right. Looking at the psychological aspects, I assume that the little organism that's being born shares in the birth process. I've always felt that my organism alone didn't control labor. It was me in conjunction with the baby that formed the birth.

J: That says a lot about relationship.

N: When my last daughter was born, she took much longer to come down the birth canal than I had expected. That's the kind of person she is. She's a Gemini. She goes, "OK, I will. No, I won't. OK, I will. No, I won't." The first part of labor was short, only fifteen minutes. When she started to come, she was, "Here I come, ready or not." Then I remember pushing with all my might, thinking, "Why doesn't this darn child emerge?" She was taking her own sweet time about it. When she got here, Tom put her on my belly, and she looked around at us with that clear seeing newborn infants have. She looked as if she were saying, "Well, here I am. I don't know about this." We all laughed.

J: What parallels do you see between the labor with your children and some of the things you and I have experienced?

N: First, I have to tell you that my name, Natalie, has something to do with birth.

J: Of course! I never thought of that!

N: I have. When I woke up to a different reality in this world, I kept experiencing myself as some sort of a mediator or gateway for many people, not just my own physical children. I secretly termed myself one of the midwives of the world. To me, this is a gift of grace. Undeserved. It's just what the One Who Knows made me. I seem to be able to let myself help certain people. When I first met you, it was easy to see that you caught hell in the group because you were the focus of the group energy quite often. I didn't know you were caesarean, and I wouldn't have thought it would make a difference. But it was clear you were having difficulty with ego boundaries, what was you and what was other.

J: I didn't know that was the difficulty. I didn't know I didn't have boundaries. I'd taken on other people's assumption that I did indeed have boundaries.

N: You do . But you manifest them differently. The birth process, contracting and pushing down through the birth canal, gives a new being a sense of "me and other." That's a whole lot of contact. Caesarean birth doesn't have that. The only "me and other" experience caesareans have is the contact of the hands of the person who lifted them out of the womb.

J: I've come to talk about it as the doctor laboring with me. It was a breakthrough when I finally understood that it was an interaction on the same level as labor. How do you see some of the things we did together as labor?

N: There were times when I experienced our relationship as one of nourisher and nourishee. In the birth experience that would have to do with those dreadful moments between the physical delivery of the child and the cutting of the umbilical cord, when the child is still being nourished by its mother even though it is external.

J: Why do you call them dreadful?

N: Because the child is external but not breathing, not yet able to sustain its own life independently. Maybe that's the midwifery I am living now, being the channel for that brief moment. After that, the little one is able to be independent.

J: In my own birth, the ether was still coming through the cord. That was a drastic time for me. It happened fast. They cut the cord before breathing got going. There was a sense of panic. I think you held me while I relived and released much of that.

In a cæsarean, the labor is being done consciously, rather than in the birth canal using ancient semi-conscious body-wisdom. What actions and attitudes do you suggest for people who will be laboring with these caesareans?

N: I haven't seen caesarean birth except on film. In them, the baby is taken out by the doctor who has gloves on, and the baby expands itself, arches its back.

J: I know that experience well.

N: That's too bad, the position that the baby is held in. The baby responds with fear. I wonder if it would be possible to take the baby out and rotate it face down so that the doctor's hands are on its belly, not its back. Even the little head could stay in contact with the mother's abdomen and chest.

J: Amazing. I had a dream a few years ago of giving birth caesarean, and that's how it happened. The baby was taken out and rolled onto my chest like that. It was a positive dream. No pain, just a lot of nourishing.

N: My impression is that caesarean babies are taken out and away. That's undoubtedly to maintain a sterile field around the incision. It must be possible to put them on the mother's chest and still maintain the sterile field.

J: I'm seeing caesarean birth as a new opportunity to let go of some of the not-so-great parts of labor and still do some parts that are necessary.

N: If the mother takes the baby on her chest and holds it, that would help. One of the things that must be present in a caesarean birth is the feeling of separation. Separation happens in a normal birth, but it is separation with the feeling of connectedness.

J: That sense of separation has forced me to go beyond my condition-ing to transpersonal levels. To know a different kind of connectedness, one that is there through physical separation. It's been one of the bonuses for me. There's a heavy illusion of separation, and also a desire to not be physically dependent on people, clinging and attached. The real gift that Ralph has given me is the experience, not just the idea, of connectedness that transcends physical separation.

N: It's been a wonderful thing in your life that you had this great need, this great experience of separation in your birth and this huge need to feel connected.

J: It's what gave me the motivation to experience this much more satisfying kind of connectedness. I'm not as dependent on physical contact, and have a lot less fear.

Do you have any other thoughts about the caesarean experience for the mother or for the child?

N: Some healing has to happen in the caesarean mother. The experi-ence of caesarean birth sets up lacks and needs in her. She has to be connected with the infant again. And she has to be connected to womankind again.

The process of delivering a child has been with us since women have been around. Out there in the boondocks, with no modern medicine, a woman puts her life on the line when she bears a child. No fooling. In the old days, it was a common story that "so and so died in childbirth. The baby's OK, but the mother didn't live."

J: That's why caesarean birth was developed.

N: Without it some of the babies wouldn't be with us, and some of the mothers wouldn't be with us. At the same time, there's a connection that has to be made, the mother-to-womankind again. something has inter-fered with the normal progression of things. No one has done anything wrong. I'm not saying that.

J: I agree. I have a lot of trouble with all this "normal and natural," the standard we are supposed to live up to, the idea that we caesareans have to make up lacks. I would rather offer the vaginal-birth learnings to caesarean mothers and caesarean children as gifts, as interesting things that might be helpful. It has to be offered in an acceptable way that doesn't make one feel wrong.

Caesarean-born people and vaginally-born people can learn some patterns and ways of being and attitudes from each other. I sometimes think of this whole caesarean thing as an experiment that the universe is using to bring a deeper level of awareness to people. One thing it does is to bring into question a lot of old, old patterns.

N: Yes, and that's going to be pretty threatening. This will be upsetting and will have some of the same emotional charge with which people will regard test-tube babies. Somewhere will be the suspicion that caesareans are not fully human.

J: Then the question comes up of what is it to be human. If to be human, you have to experience the journey down the birth canal, then we caesareans are not human. You're then faced with either saying we're not fully human or of letting go of some of your preconceptions and body sense of what it is to be human. It is going to force a transcendence of some deeply ingrained patterns.

More comments by Natalie, two years later (August 1984):

I have been talking to several friends about this book. They ask me what you are trying to do. I've been saying things like: "The primary experience of birth, being drastically different for caesareans, gives them a different kind of world view. A unique experience. Jane has found this manifests in subtle ways. She feels somehow different, as pears and apples are different."

That statement has set people's minds working. They go right into seeing how it means an expansion of our definition of humanity, and how that is becoming more and more necessary with test-tube babies, frozen sperm and so on. This question of what is human has become important. People are talking about fetal rights and all kinds of strange things we don't know how to deal with

My thinking about all this is that the issue is to big too handle. But we are comfortable now with the idea of caesarean birth. It is a non-threatening place to begin to ask the questions about differences, about what is human. Are we different because of different birth experiences?

Interview with Tom Ednie *M.D., (psychiatrist)*   July 4, 1982

Tom Ednie, M.D., vaginally first-born, American Scot and husband of Natalie Ednie, is the father of seven. He served as anesthetist for many caesareans. A senior Flight Surgeon, he received the U.S. Air Force Commendation Medal as chief of its largest neuropsychiatric treatment center. He has travelled in five continents, been a psychiatric inpatient, and studied with diverse teachers including Leslie Farber, Huston Smith, Fritz Perls, Stan Grof and American Indian shamans. He now practices psychiatry in Sandpoint, Idaho.

Knowing Tom and sharing our inner journeys helped me greatly with the process of healing the inner splits between helper and helpee, obstetrician

*and baby, and theoretical knowledge and experiential knowing. He is the
first psychiatrist I ever hugged!*

J: Five years ago, when you were teaching courses on philosophy and
religion, you invited me to present my caesarean material. It was the first
time I had ever shared publicly what I have been doing with caesarean
birth. You saw a connection between the work I am doing on the
experience of being born caesarean, and philosophy and religion.

T: The birth experience ties together religion and philosophy. What set
me off on this is a connection I learned from anthropologist/philosopher
Gregory Bateson. He said that you can't have an integrated world-view if
your idea of "what things are" is based on separate theories of knowledge
from your understanding of "how things change."

J: You split yourself if they aren't.

T: Exactly. You split the world. You split yourself. With words we define
things as separate. We define the boundaries. This is this, and over against
it is something that is different. When we use verbal language everything is
already divided up. So basically all we can talk about is what things are and
what things are not. And we can't really talk about how they become what
they are. Yet how things become is pretty important. But we all do have in
us a feel for how things become, and it is a bodily, physical thing. We have
all gone through the experience of birth before we even had words. And
then we go through the experience of growing and lots of other transitions
that are physical processes. Being hungry, then being not hungry, etc.

J: Would it be accurate to say that the first language we learn is body
language?

T: Yes. Body language. We later tack words onto it.

J: Words, especially in the English language, are about definite things
and not about how they change. But then, there are verbs.

T: But our verbs are what the things do. Or they are *being* verbs like, "I
am hungry," or, "I *am* not hungry." And there again we don't have words
to describe even that kind of transition, except, "I am a little bit hungry."

J: And one of the ways you learn the body language is in the birth
process. This is amazing. Here I am describing caesarean birth with a
verbal language that has its roots in a body language created by vaginally-
born people. So I am trying to use the language of vaginal birth, the
language of a culture that has its roots in that process. I'm trying to
translate, I guess. Trying to translate my experience into a language that is
based on the vaginal-birth experience.

T: A language that is based on a different kind of experience from yours.
We get our feel for change, I think, from experiences in early life. If, as
many psychologists have pointed out, your birth experience is your
paradigm for change, then having caesarean birth will give you a whole
different paradigm for what change is and how it happens. Not the long,
draw-out process we are accustomed to.

J: You have talked generally about how the birth process is one of the roots of language—body language and then vèrbal language. Can you say something about how the specifics of the pattern I presented in the slide show fit into this general structure?

T: What emerged for me was the uniqueness of the experience you were portraying. We have this category of "normal" vaginal birth and the category of caesarean birth. What came through was that yours was a unique experience. Yours was not an experience of a category. Categories are imposed later.

J: Every vaginal birth is also unique. There are, however, similarities among them, and language and culture grow on the similarities. For a long time I thought I should make generalizations about caesarean birth that didn't include the particular little quirks of my own birth. But I have realized that I have to understand the particulars of mine, then move on to seeing the particulars of other caesareans, and then see what commonalities there are among us. There are going to be as many differences as there are commonalities.

T: That sounds like a reasonable western approach. What we're aiming at in most academic disciplines is the general, over-all law, the highest of abstractions in which we can capture the truth. But what I am saying is that what is *real* is the absolutely unique. Without the unique, there would be no general law. When you point out the value of appreciation of differences, you are pointing in the direction of uniqueness rather than toward abstractions.

J: I hope I am creating a scaffolding for caesareans to stand on so they won't feel quite so lost along the way. My ambivalence around doing this is that I don't want to create a structure that people will use to block their own unique experience.

T: It would be a mistake to take the usual scientific approach to this, just find the abstractions and throw out all the uniqueness.

J: That understanding grows from the balance of your theoretical understanding of philosophy and religion with your day to day contact with patients.

T: That's what got my interest started in all this. Trying to get them into diagnostic categories that I'd learned from books, I found so often, namely every time, that they don't fit.

J: What was the use for you of these categories? Given that they never really fit, what is the usefulness of the categories?

T: The usefulness is that, in general, growth involves establishing a structure based on the theory of knowledge you have at the time. Further growth, death/rebirth, involves transcending that structure. You've got to stand on it first before you can transcend it.

J: So a caesarean-born person needs first to come in contact with what their patterns are, and how they've used them as building blocks in their life. Then they can begin to move beyond them. There probably will be points along the way when people are attached to their birth pattern.

I've noticed caesareans tend not to know how to push through barriers and break out of structures.

T: That certainly fits with my experience of you a few years back. You were very stuck. I didn't understand it. What were you holding on to? Now it seems clear that you weren't holding on; you were waiting for a savior to come along, because that's what happened in birth.

J: I had learned that some external thing was going to come and do it for me. I vacillated between waiting for someone to do it for me and gritting my teeth, being stubbornly independent, saying, "I can do it all by myself." The way out for me has been a transcendence, a transpersonal kind of experience. Knowing that the "I," small me, can't do it all alone no matter how hard I try, but neither is a separate "someone" always going to come in and save me. The way out of this difficulty is to experience that we are all connected with each other, to experience a mystical oneness.

T: That hooks it right up with religion. I saw you as waiting for a savior. The experience of waiting for a savior is found in most religions.

J: When I see a behavior in myself and in another caesarean, first it seems that we do it because we are caesarean. The I get a feeling, "Everyone does this, so what is the big deal?" I call the patterns caesarean; then I say they're not caesarean.

T: You are saying that the difference between caesarean and non-caesarean is not an end point; it needs to be understood, integrated and transcended. But what do you transcend it to? It seems to me that you transcend it to the knowing on which our bodies are based on. The stuff in our genes.

J: So it goes beyond birth, behind birth to a body language that is cellular.

T: It goes to a level that I think might be identified with the oneness of everything.

J: I remember the first time I consciously was aware of that oneness. There wasn't any me, and there wasn't anything out there. There was just consciousness and various ways of dividing it up so it could be experienced. Part of why I do this work is that I am interested in creating a map that will help caesarean people. I also am creating the map to show by contrast the vaginal birth map, and to say we have to go deeper to find our common human experience. Going deeper is a step in the direction of experiencing the awareness of unity or oneness.

My hope is that people will see beyond the pieces of my journey and allow the material to resonate with their own experience. That's all communication is. The external form, the words and the pictures are not "it." They are something used to evoke in other people awareness of their own experience.

You were saying that you were fascinated by the religious implications. Say some more about that.

T: It seems as if the savior we all wait for is to be found in the direction of uniqueness, rather than in the direction of generalizations and abstractions. We get out of the splits between body and mind by moving in the direction of uniqueness.

J: When you feel crazy, it's often because your unique experience doesn't fit into the pattern that you think you're supposed to fit it into. The way out isn't to fit it into the patterns more, but to honor your experience.

T: We come to that by finding that we don't fit; no matter what we do, we do not fit. Whereupon we give up and discover that it is OK to be unique. And it seems to me that the savior comes along in this discovery that, "I am this unique person, and that's OK. If it weren't OK, I wouldn't be."

J: So the feeling of being not OK, of needing a savior, is connected with the anxiety that comes up around not fitting into "the way things are supposed to be." And when you come home, find out who you really are, it isn't that there's a separate part of yourself, a savior, that comes from somewhere. It's more that feeling saved comes in letting go of attempting to measure up to something that you don't fit.

I'm interested in how we apply what we've been talking about to therapy. What specific suggestions would you give to a vaginally-born therapist, working with a caesarean-born client? What would you suggest to a therapist working with a caesarean-born person who was in the kind of state I was in a few years ago?

T: The only valid suggestions that I would have is that therapists go through these kinds of experiences themselves in terms of their own birth. I don't think they are equipped to deal with this until they have. You can't share an experience you haven't experienced.

J: What you are talking about is the training of therapists. That goes a level deeper than just giving them a recipe for dealing with caesareans. What happens for caesareans is that we are forced to this depth because so much mainstream culture is based on the vaginal-birth process. We don't fit. Any of the therapies that try to make us fit in just make us more crazy. We don't have the pattern they are trying to fit us into.

T: That may be a good suggestion to therapists, to recognize that theories of what is going on with people are based on a paradigm that may not fit. I have to emphasize that a lot of therapy goes on without confronting that level, but therapy in general deals with people who feel they don't fit somehow or other.

J: This connects with the experience of some of my caesarean-born friends. They went through a lot of therapy, got hospitalized, shock treatments, the whole thing. They were being treated for cultural misfit, but neither they nor the therapists knew it. They didn't have the awareness that a lot of culture is based on vaginal birth patterns, and these caesarean people didn't fit. Maybe one of the messages of this work is that you've got to go deeper.

T: If you want to put it in those terms, most therapists need to be pointed beyond psychology to philosophy, and beyond that into religion and mystical experiences. That's where it all comes from, unique experience.

Interview with Rosemary Hayes (*caesarean-born therapist/artist*)
July 12, 1982

Rosemary Hayes grew up in Washington and has a degree in psychology. She is married and has three children.

She designed and made jewelry, studied history of art, and got an MA degree in counseling. A therapist, she is studying at the Gestalt Institute of San Francisco. Her current interest is in image making and the healing process.

Rosemary and I share a language of symbols. While we have different artistic styles, we found with great excitement the first time we compared images that we had in similar ways expressed the dynamics of caesarean birth.

J: When I first saw your paintings a year ago, I sensed that you speak the same visual language I do. Both your and my images go way beyond the birth process; they are archetypal. But it is useful to look at them in relation to the birth process. I say that because I don't want to diminish your images by stuffing them into the conceptual framework I am using. They are archetypal, and they are also relevant to birth, because birth is how the universal becomes particular, personal and individual.

R: This one of the wound (*See Figure 15*) will be probably the most relevant, at a conscious level, to your work. This painting was three months in process. It was started on my fortieth birthday. I had gone to the mountains in the morning alone, all dressed in white to do a healing ritual and to celebrate my passage to forty. I remember looking at my life. I felt I wasn't growing. At some point in the day I realized I had a wound. The wound was me. I saw this open hole. Energy had been draining out of me all the time. There was a visual sense and also a kinesthetic sense that my front was this wound. It was so vivid, and I'd never had it before. Focusing on it, I realized that I wasn't wounded, but my mother had been wounded. That's the first time at a kinesthetic level that I had any sense of being caesarean. Once, in therapy, I knew mentally that I needed to recreate

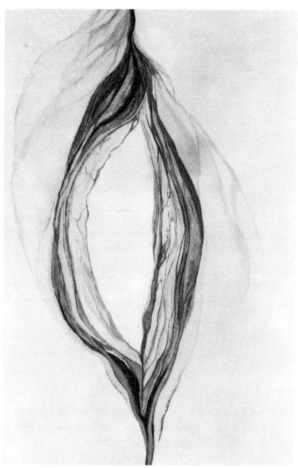

Figure 15—The Wound (by Rosemary Hayes)

being born. But that was an intellectual knowing. During the day alone, I somehow got myself separated from the wound. I realized that I was whole. I had taken on my mother's woundedness. That related to the caesarean birth and to a lot of other things. In my vision, the wound was all red. It was so powerful to paint. I didn't want anyone to know I was painting a wound, so I painted it blue.

I was going an internship in family therapy. I was in constant pain and anxiety over it. One night a couple of Ph.D.'s, some others and I arranged ourselves in a circle. I looked at this man. He's about 6'3", a Ph.D. from Stanford. I wanted to push him to the wall. No one else was acting that way.

I looked at him and said, "I want to push you." He invited me to do it. I planted my feet and began pushing. I pushed and pushed, and he pushed against me. At one point I thought he was going to pick me up off the ground. I felt total rage, like, "If you dare to change the rules, I could kill you." He didn't do it. He quit. He was stunned by my strength. The energy entered my body.

J: He'd been willing to labor with you. Does that fit at all?

R: It fits absolutely. I had all this power. I knew when I got home that I had gone through something. The next day, I painted the pink and rose part. The flesh. I had never painted like that. The paint knew where to go, and I loved the painting. The bright red was done after I did the pinks. I had more courage to show that it was a wound.

J: I was interested in what you said about the man picking you up. That struck me as being like birth, a man taking away all of your control of the situation.

R: He was strong enough to do that. I knew I'd feel like killing him. I know that this is definitely related to your caesarean work.

J: When I saw that painting the first time, something clicked in me. You were talking about it as a wound, but not as connected with birth. I came up to you afterward and said, "Hey, that's a birth opening, too." You knew, but you hadn't said it. Then you told me you were caesarean.

R: An important thing I haven't taken the time to work out is that the wound is in my mother, not in me.

J: You two weren't differentiated then. Birth creates that differentiation. So you have been creating the differentiation for the first time. Letting go of the wound that you were carrying around.

R: I have experienced myself in life as a wounded one.

J: I think that the physiological and biochemical changes that are the mother's response to the cutting are also felt in the baby's body. Even though there is anesthesia, there is still reaction, but the mother isn't aware of it consciously.

R: That makes a lot of sense to me.

J: I have noticed how your images are both about your physical birth and your spiritual rebirth. It's important for me to remember that I'm not talking just about reliving birth and releasing some of the distortions and habits learned there. This work is larger than that. Perhaps in our physical birth we learn in our bodies a dynamic that gives us tools, images, procedures, dances and maps that guide us in the process of spiritual rebirth. Rather than looking at the birth experience in the Freudian sense as a "trauma," we can see it in a much more positive way as important learning about how to change, to make transition, to go to another level.

R: That's true. The healing of the physical and psychological comes from a spiritual place for me.

Figure 16—The Firebird (by Rosemary Hayes)

J: Often when people look at caesarean birth from just the physical and psychological perspectives, they want to fix up the caesarean-born people to make them be like vaginally-born, "normal" people. From the spiritual perspective, you see that both kinds of birth learning are material to transcend, as well as tools to use, in going to a higher level.

R: I did this painting of a stark tree and a bird made of fire (*See Figure 16*) when I was sick in bed with the flu, and I felt quite ill. There was a lot of emotional stuff. I remember being aware that I was capable of murder. I remember a lot of anger and pain. When I painted this, I was in intense emotional pain.

J: I put this at the place in the birth where you are in the hands of the doctor. You mentioned that you felt you could kill when you thought the man was going to lift you up. In the birth, this is the place where you have

Figure 17—Butterfly (by Rosemary Hayes)

just been lifted up, and there is intense anger. A nurse friend of mine says she sees caesarean babies come out very angry.

R: Until the time with him, I wasn't aware of that anger in myself.

J: It was a memory.

R: I don't know when I painted this one of a butterfly and tree rising out of a flower. (*See Figure 17*) As I was painting the root lines of the flower, I realized that the roots penetrating the flower were rape. In a quiet way, this painting contained violence. I would paint these things and not be trying to communicate anything, but the thoughts would come after the painting.

J: That's how it was for me, too, like art therapy, the use of the symbols to evoke things. Once you told me that you understood the penetration, the rape of the flower, as what was necessary. The mother, the flower, had to be cut in order that the daughter, the butterfly be released.

Figure 18—Fire Tree (by Rosemary Hayes)

R: This one of fire rising through the center of tree (*See Figure 18*) is mystical to me, about mystical union.

J: The tree and the fire are one at this point.

R: The fire is inner and outer there. I have a definite physical sensation as I look at it now. Openness. And there's knowing that the fire does not consume. It feels like dying, but it isn't.

J: When the fire was separate with the firebird, it was pain. This is integration. It is like my lighted shadow dream and painting. (*See Part II, May 27, 1979 and Figure 9*)

R: See the Buddha shape of the fire at the top of the next painting? (*See Figure 19*) I saw that shape in a dream. The message in the dream was,

Figure 19—Buddha (by Rosemary Hayes)

"Paint this." I said, "No, that's a Buddhist image, and it's been done before." Then in the dream, the fire was brought right up to me. It was like, "You don't get to choose. You paint it." I'd never had anything like that. Just the top part was in the dream. Then, as usual, a tree grew there.

J: It is the most free, complete tree you have. It reaches down to earth, your first earth in these paintings. I connect it to my dream (*See Part II, July 27, 1979 and Figure 10*) of the golden sun-god pressing me into the earth, giving me the opportunity to experience and release all the fear, hurt, anger and pain connected with caesarean birth, healing myself.

Interview with Bruce King and Marilee James King (*vaginally-born/caesarean-born couple*) July 23, 1982.

Bruce and Marilee King are marriage, family and child counselors. They are partners in a transpersonally oriented group psychotherapy practice and referral network in the San Francisco Bay Area called "A Resource for Change."

This conversation with Bruce and Marilee confirmed for me what I had suspected—that a deep relationship between a caesarean-born person and a vaginally-born person has unique difficulties and special opportunities.

J: Marilee said that you, Bruce, might have some interesting thoughts on being intimate with a non-labor caesarean whose birth learning is different from yours. The dance one does in birth is a prototype for later relationship patterns. At that level, you two do different dances. This difference is an opportunity in the therapy context when a caesarean-born person and a vaginally-born person work together, and I think it is even more so in a couple relationship. To find your common ground, you both have to transcend identifying with your birth learning. You have to go deeper to find your common place. To the extent that you are each identified with your birth learning, there will be conflicts and, "My way is right. Your way is wrong." You can take that conflict and turn it into an opportunity to disidentify with the birth learning you have and to go beyond right/wrong.

B: The idea of a caesarean birth being different from a vaginal birth occurred to us fairly early in our relationship. As lovers do, we began to talk about who we were, and at some point, Marilee said she was non-labor caesarean. Before that, my only experience with caesarean was through Shakespeare. Macbeth. "Not of woman born." I was curious about the meaning of being caesarean. I remember Marilee saying, "I wonder if some of the things I am experiencing in my life, areas where I get entangled with other people, have anything to do with my caesarean birth."

M: This was all before I saw your slide show.

B: When she saw you were doing a presentation last year, she'd said, "I've got to go to that." When she came back, she was very excited. It was an opening for both of us. There was corroboration for our previous thoughts.

J: Do you remember any of the particulars?

B: With a caesarean, you mobilize this whole team to do it for you. I had been amazed at Marilee's ability to draw together diverse people and pull something off. . .conferences, classes, various things. It was one of the first things that attracted me to her.

M: I thought of something that we went through in our relationship. Remember when we were in London sitting by the Thames?

B: Yes.

M: It was the first time we'd lived together. We'd been lovers for a while, were very much in love, and went to Europe. Remember the tangles we'd get into? It seems like it had to do with birth learning. Sitting by the Thames we were really at an impasse in our relationship. I tried to tell you what I wanted, and you were trying to tell me I don't know what. It felt like we were at that impasse of a different kind of a learning and knowing. Not that what we wanted was different, but that where we were and how we'd go there was totally different. I won't ever forget how it felt. I just wanted to be there in relation to you, Bruce, and that was much too fast for you, too deep, too soon.

B: Early in our relationship, we reached a point where I had to back off a little. It was much too fast.

J: What were your feelings at that point, Marilee? Because I know how I react to that kind of situation.

M: Very frustrated and thinking that what I needed to do was to continue to insist, rather than knowing how to pull back. What I did do, though, was to remove myself at those times. Physically pull away rather than emotionally pull away.

B: In other relationships I'd had, the relationship would go and then cease and then go. A stop/start. That, to me, is development.

J: That sounds like labor!

B: With Marilee, it seemed like an uninterrupted happening.

J: Total and all at once.

B: My relationship to Marilee has helped me to see that there don't always have to be barriers. I usually get through them, but there's more struggle involved. Marilee will say "Try looking at it this way." That has helped me attain goals and in my daily life. Marilee didn't have a strong sense of starting from point A and, after some length of time, ending up at point B. The future wasn't something she gave a lot of consideration to, at least in the sense that I did. She has a way in life that I don't have, and I have a way in life that she doesn't. We have focused on our differences and similarities and what we can do with those. It has strengthened our relationship.

When we're stuck, we ask, "Who can do this the best?"

J: You have different resources. Some of it is the birth and some other experiences. Maybe the different birth patterns helped you focus on differences.

M: And how to use those differences.

B: When you did that guided imagery journey and got that image of a wall, that was good for me. The not struggling through but getting people on the other side to help.

J: Does that image help you to understand her process?

B: Yes. My way is to go through it. I was expecting her to push through. That works for me, but I see there's a softer way. There are people who are willing to help, so why come out of a situation bruised?

J: The caesarean can learn the possibility of pushing through. But it has to be offered as a possibility, rather than "You should push through." What is better for a vaginally-born person to say is, "Here's something I learned in my birth. It worked for me. It might work for you."

B: If I push Marilee, she goes slower. Not out of stubbornness, but what that brings up in her is confusion, makes her scattered. If I explain or just demonstrate, it is fine.

M: One thing that continually comes back to me is your drawing of the birthday party. All these people seem to be giving you gifts they learned in their birth process.

J: They are laboring with me.

M: The one who is giving you open space is amazing to me.

J: He's also caesarean. He knew enough to give me space and not to come at me with something. I put the ring in his hand intuitively when I did the drawing. I didn't consciously do it to symbolize space.

M: In many instances in my life, laboring happens after the birth of something. Labor comes after birth.

J: Labor is still going on for me.

B: I've noticed that often when you tell people about this work, they have a hard time.

J: In what way?

B: There's fear there. A fear of someone making a big deal out of the way they were born, particularly caesarean. Caesarean is still pretty charged. There's a cut involved and something considered unnatural.

J: There's a huge emotional charge about this, a lot of negative emotion about caesarean birth. Stan Grof made the point that in psychiatric literature, there are many, many articles on the finest details of the trauma of toilet training, but, until recently, nothing about the immensely more powerful experience of being born caesarean. He wondered if this was perhaps because caesarean birth was too emotionally charged for even those professionals. I'm not surprised that you, Marilee, had some doubt after our last talk. You, too, were running into all this. Going against the flow of a culture that is somewhat based on vaginal birth.

M: That reminds me of when we talked about caesareans coming together, experiencing each other. Let us be together and see what comes up. Given that we are different, how do we relate to and transform the world?

J: You, Bruce, mentioned that you were aware of differences between your way and her way, and you give one specific about your wanting expansion and contraction in relationship. Are there any others that came up for you?

B: What she brought me to was my essence. That was a strong point of attraction. We had a stormy courtship, to say the least. One of the things that drew us together was that, with Marilee, I could, much more than before, tap the essential being. That might be related to how she was born.

J: Does that connect, Marilee, to what you are saying. You made the distinction between identifying with something external and with your inner being. It sounds like he is saying the same thing in a different language.

M: Yes. I think that's a quality that I bring, and not from an ego level, but from a place that says, "I am." I find it in my teaching and in my therapy, too. When I am fully being who I am and not pretending, it happens in the other person, too.

B: The flip side of that ability is that it is also a vulnerable space. I feel very protective of Marilee when she is vulnerable. We have done some workshops together. If she is leading the group, and the group is right there, the energy is fantastic. People say it was like a religious experience. But I perceive two areas of danger. One is, if someone blocks it, the level at which that person can be vicious toward the person channeling is incredible. More subtle and dangerous is what happens afterwards. After they've been in that open space, people sometimes panic. They take that fear and turn it onto the innocent being and become devouring. You've just tamed a pack of beasts, the beast that is in all of us, and then one suddenly attacks with no apparent reason.

J: That fits in with the boundaries issue caesareans seem to have. Knowing how to let go of boundaries and unify with another, but not being as good at separating. As I learn to separate, I can choose when to be open. I don't take on the group energy so unconsciously.

In the workshop situation, you are a giver of an initiation, and that means you have to be able to follow up on it. That's the hardest part. Initiation is a first step, bringing people into awareness of a new level of consciousness. So many traditions are built around the question, "What do you do after the initiation?"

I think of the experience I had of feeling my heart open when touched on the chest by another caesarean person. Afterwards neither of us knew what to do with what I was feeling. Neither he nor I knew how to handle the attachment I felt toward him.

M: Was he the man who is giving you the circle in the birthday party drawing?

J: Yes. He was uncomfortable with my attachment after that touch. It was only several years later that I understood that he had given me an initiation. I'm not sure he understood it at the time either.

M: Caesarean people are perhaps doorways, at a different octave in life, not better, just different. At a different place on the spectrum of consciousness because of different birth learning. Therefore, we initiate that vibration when we connect with others. So there will be initiations.

B: It is interesting what you say about an initiation. That rings true. It might be what happened in our relationship. Through Marilee, I had an opening I was looking for. For a long time, I didn't know what that was about at all. That probably had a lot to do with the difficulties we have experienced in coming together as a couple. Tremendous resistance on my part particularly, except that something always drew me back to why I met this woman. It could be that I was seeking a follow-up to the initiation, and neither of us had a form for that follow-up, and have subsequently evolved it through the last few years. I feel we have been exploring why we are together.

Another thing that has helped me is looking at the question, "If caesarean birth is this way, what is vaginal birth?" It has provided me with an opening for looking at my own birth process. I mentioned earlier that a sense of struggle is there for me. Now I relate it to my birth process. What your work unlocks in me is itself as revolutionary as the caesarean stuff.

J: I am as interested in the light that this shines on other birth patterns as I am in the caesarean material itself. It is an opportunity for all of us to back off from our birth learning and find out what it is to be human.

B: When I talked to a group of people about your work not everybody there knew about it. I said that the seed of it comes from Stan Grof's work, the birth process being one's life process. That statement made all the difference in the world. People were saying, "Oh, another way to look at one's way in the world." There needed to be an indentifiable hook, and then people were willing to take another look.

I think that the population at large doesn't mean to be negative about caesarean birth, but it doesn't know any other way. It sees something foreign, something that disturbs the status quo.

J: It brings into awareness their own birth patterns. When you look at Stan's work, you see that vaginal birth is intense, too.

Thoughts on being born caesarean—Dennis McCracken   July 25, 1982

Dennis McCracken earns his living as a clinical social worker for Kaiser-Permanente health program. His career is being a student of how we individually and collectively create reality.

Having had only the briefest conversation with him at a conference, I was delighted Dennis independently recorded his thoughts about being caesarean. The similarities to my experience and to that of other caesareans are striking.

I am recording these remarks as I am getting ready to see your slide show. This is my last chance to record my pristine and uninfluenced remarks before I see what you have to say about the experience of being born caesarean.

My mother always stressed how easy the birth was for her, and I always assumed it had been the same for me. Whenever I heard speculations about the trauma of birth, I always assumed it didn't apply to me.

I didn't get a hint about anything peculiar about the way I came into this world until I was an experimental subject of Helen Wambach in her massive past-life recall study. In one trip that was devoted to looking at this life, we were going to relive the birth experience.

I was prepared for an easy entry, but it felt like an abrupt transition that was totally unexpected. I was in a comfortable place, pleasantly neutral, when all of a sudden, I was grabbed and yanked into the cold. Moved around experiencing disequilibrium. I can't describe it. I am reliving it at the moment. Feel that my self has been diminished suddenly against my will, victimized.

As I just now recalled that rebirth experience, I had a flash of numerous occasions as a child in which I experienced that startle response. It is a nerve-jarring, total body response that I literally had trained myself out of by the time I was an adolescent. Any situation in which my equilibrium was disturbed, being awakened suddenly, any startle would arouse in me that total body response.

After I first talked briefly with you, I began speculating about other effects. One of the elements of my personality that may be related to my caesarean birth is a dreaminess or unearthliness, as though I never really touched earth. Perhaps this is one of the reasons I chose to be born that way. It was a switch from one form of reality to another, like flipping a switch with no sense of "being born" or of struggling, or putting any effort into it, or desiring to escape the compression that I've heard from others who describe their birth memories. One of the other effects may be my continuous struggle to deal with struggle. I don't like to struggle. Everything is supposed to be easy, as it is in the other world in which we think something and it is so. Where we aren't troubled by the passage of time or things needing the development and concentration which are necessary in the physical plane.

As a child I had some disturbing experiences around what probably seemed to be lying to others. I had to learn that what was in my mind wasn't reality in this plane, this ordinary reality. I had some confrontations with those who had a perception of reality that was quite different from mine. I have a feeling it took me longer to learn the rules of what it means to be real than perhaps it did for others.

I do well as a short-term therapist with my clients, sensing quickly what their major problems are. I home in quickly on those aspects of the situation or personality that need immediate attention. I can quickly shift gears with people. I am also good at sensing when the time is ripe for a quantum leap. I feel I can see these choice points because of my lack of ties to sensate reality. Indeed, my most poorly developed and most unconscious function is the sensate or practical, which is the one that grounds me in reality. The whole focus of my second half of life is to develop that earthbound quality, to put my feet on the ground.

×○×○×○×○×○×○×○×○×○×○×○×○×○×○×○×○×○×

Comments by Jody Longnecker after she read my article "Caesarean Birth and Psychotherapy" and a transcript of my lecture/slide show. October 12, 1982.

I met Jody soon after she moved to New Hampshire. We sat on her porch having a drink, getting acquainted and looking at the mountains. She asked what I was doing. "Writing a book on being born caesarean," I replied. She exclaimed, "I am a caesarean, too. What have you learned about caesareans?" I started telling her about the relationship pattern of wanting to go all the way in immediately, or else getting scared and running away. She started finishing sentences for me. I said, "You know!" She said, "I've been doing that all my life. You mean I am not crazy?"

Hearing this from a person who had never been particularly interested in psychology was a real affirmation for me.

Dear Jane,

I found your articles fascinating—who isn't interested in reading about themselves?

Your list of habits, expectations and patterns in "Caesarean Birth and Psychotherapy" got to me on all counts. I have always been hyper-

—118—

sensitive; and defensive. Mother always told me not to be so sensitive. And I have a touch problem. I also get neck pain before I even realize I'm uptight. Always on the left side.

We hadn't discussed the dependence quality before. As a matter of fact, I hadn't recognized it as such in myself till I read this paper. I am frequently considered a "strong" person, in charge, etc. Yet if anyone will take the lead or make decisions, I back off with relief. It's easier for me to do it someone else's way even if I might think it is wrong. I let others take charge by abdicating my responsibility, not by asking for help. I don't unload on someone; I just get out of the way. I also resent having the decision-making responsibility put on me, almost to the point of self-pity.

Having been delivered by a male obstetrician (not many female M.D.s in those days), I jumped at your statement about distorted relationships with such people. I have not until very recently been able to have a friendship with a man. I have alway felt compelled to spar and fence with men, behaving aggressively and all the while considering them from the sex angle, not as people.

Friendships for me don't develop. They either are or they aren't. I am abruptly and immediately attracted to people. I don't think I "get to know" them. Those few friends are very important to me.

As for goals, I've never had any and am in awe of those who discuss their goals and their actions in relation to goals. I feel stupid for not having developed goals in spite of the fact that I'm supposed to have accomplished a lot of things.

Yes, I have always assumed help would be there when I needed it.

Your remarks are helpful to me in understanding my tendency to be overly direct and outspoken, even to the point of upsetting the listener. As my daughter says, "Mom, you come on too strong." I try to remember this and "cool it" but am not always successful.

As I've said many times, you have opened a fascinating new line of thought for which I shall always be grateful.

Sincerely,
Jody

Conversation with Sandy Hastings (*potential mother of a caesarean child*)
November 3, 1982.

Sandy Hastings is not caesarean born. Her interest in caesarean birth
stems from surgery she had which will make it necessary for her children
to be born caesarean. She is also interested in the transformative aspects
of a birth experience which is not as physically violent as vaginal birth.
Sandy grew up in western Oregon and has lived in the Bay Area for
twenty years. She is the librarian at the California Institute of Trans-
personal Psychology in Menlo Park. She is married to Arthur Hastings.

As a person actively embracing and living a transpersonal perspective on
life, Sandy affirmed for me the larger implications of caesarean birth. On
the other hand, being a woman who has had surgery and whose children
will have to be born caesarean, she was able to help me connect this
larger perspective back to the specifics of a physical body.

J: It is about a year since we first talked, and I showed you my slide
show. One thing you said keeps echoing in my mind. It was a perspective I
had never heard before. You talked about how the work ethic, the need to
struggle in order to feel OK, doesn't fit well with what the world is evolving
to. The caesarean's sense of not struggling fits better.

S: In the next ten or twenty years so much is going to be done by
computer; it will be so easy. The idea of going out and wrestling your living
from your environment is not going to be a valid model. Coming into the
world with that struggle model is going to have less survival value. If we
don't change our concepts about that, I think we are going to run out of our
resources. If we think, "abundance," instead of "scarcity," it is going to
happen. The minute you get a concept for something, you can do it. Like
the people who broke the four-minute mile. As soon as one did it, many
people did it. The idea that you have to struggle is part of the scarcity
model.

There may be some reason for caesarean birth beyond what we see
when we look at the medical picture. We see doctors and hospitals that are
scared to death of being sued. We see a society that, as soon as it gets a
technology, uses it. But there may be some survival reason on another
level. The idea of being without boundaries may be exactly what we need.
We need to see the world without boundaries.

J: Recently I have come to understand that you can quite quickly make
tremendous changes in consciousness, the caesarean thing of going all at
once rather than in waves as in labor. But you can't do it all by yourself.
The rugged individual model doesn't work for taking these great leaps. In
the caesarean pattern, one first feels intruded upon. Then one is lifted up
with love. I first came to a deep understanding of that while I was in a
rebirthing session. I went from, "I need so much help, and that's not OK,"

to accepting the help, then on to a sense of everyone experiencing that interconnectedness and interdependence. I saw that we can make tremendous changes when we work together. I'd heard that intellectually before, but this was a deeper experience of it. It is part of my birth learning, my native culture.

S: What's needed is a feeling of national boundaries not being there. I think that national boundaries start from body boundaries.

J: You need to have boundaries be an option rather than an absolute reality. Boundaries are useful sometimes. It is not OK to be too merged with everything without knowing that's what you are doing. I think the non-labor caesarean has some problems with being merged with everything without knowing it, because of not knowing the experience of boundaries very well.

S: I wonder if it isn't much harder to start with boundaries and try to experience having no boundaries.

J: You know what came up again? "Different." Just different. I don't know if it is easier or harder.

The other day a friend said to me that caesareans get to choose consciously their bonding with the earth. We get to choose with full awareness, rather than having it happen to us in birth. Some caesareans I've met have talked about that. I am beginning to look beyond the personal and psychological aspects. Caesareans are a different tribe or clan.

S: It will be interesting to see how the balance tips as we see the effect of having so many children born caesarean.

J: I've been told that in some South American countries it is 40 to 50 percent.

One thing I want to ask you about is what it is like to be cut open. As the child, I experienced it to the extent that I was unified with my mother. But there is still a lot of deep cellular fear around being cut. The cutting is one of the things that scares people about caesarean birth.

S: When you are cut open, there is such an immediate awareness of vulnerable body, which you don't have if you're not broken into that way.

J: In your surgery, you were awake?

S: No I was asleep. But I certainly felt the vulnerability afterwards. I felt like my guts were going to fall out. I think caesarean birth would be a difficult experience for the mother. It isn't a struggle for her, either. It's not a pushing out. It is being broken into.

J: In a vaginal birth, both the mother and child are active as well as receptive. In a caesarean, the doctor is the active one.

S: The mother is an uninvolved third party.

J: I was talking about this with my mother a couple of weeks ago. Her comment was that she doesn't know anything about caesarean birth. She was just out of it.

S: A lot of women feel that way about vaginal birth, especially the generation of our mothers. They were put out totally, and they don't want to know anything more about it. Despite the fact that even non-caesarean birth has been treated as a sickness by the medical profession, most women usually believe that it is natural. But a caesarean is surgery; and surgery is strange. It is so far removed from our beginnings. Giving birth vaginally today still happens in basically the same way as it did 500 years ago. The changes are superficial. But caesarean is different. People born vaginally could have been born under any circumstances. But every caesarean-born person knows birth would not have happened except for this special technique which is not "natural." What are the implications of that in terms of states of consciousness? Here's a soul that, except for that special technique, would have had to come around again.

J: It would have died in birth, maybe killing the mother, too.

S: Unconsciously these people know that without a hospital, a doctor and people trained in certain techniques, they would not have survived.

J: I think it is accepting your dependence and trusting other people

S: I think it is a merging of the technological culture and the natural culture. A bridge. What that means is that we can't do without technology. We can't go back.

J: Whenever I hear anti-technology talk, I remember that I wouldn't be here without that technology.

S: You know it consciously because you have done a lot of work on it. Hundreds and thousands of caesareans don't know it consciously but feel it. They have that gut feeling, and they are reacting. It makes a difference. What does it mean in terms of society that a large pool of people, in the usual birth method, were not meant to survive? In some way the old program was not intended to be carried out.

J: In one of my meditations I tuned into all the beings who had tried to come through the birth canal and whose heads were too big. All the ones who had to abandon the structure they had been creating for nine months and try over again. It is hard to describe my experience. There was a lot of fear and a lot of love I felt for my work with caesarean birth. I have thought of what caesarean birth means in an evolutionary sense. Now we can have bigger heads, larger brains and all that implies.

S: We've had to leave at nine months. Otherwise, our heads would be too big. What would it mean if we could stay in longer?

J: We are taking some of the restrictions off. I see that as a two-edged sword. When you take a restriction off and give people more freedom, they can use it wisely or foolishly.

One of the people at my slide show in Colorado at the rebirthing conference was a woman who has had four caesareans, and the last one was a non-labor. She is having problems with that 10 year old. The girl has been called hyperactive. I suggested that possibly she still has to labor with that girl. I wonder if you have thought about that in looking ahead to having a caesarean child. What is the relationship going to be between you and that child?

Stan Grof talks about the intensity of labor. It is a life-or-death situation. It is the most intense thing people ever experience. So if this woman is actually laboring with her child now, she should not be surprised that it is intense. and she shouldn't be so hard on herself for having to relate intensely with her child. She is giving her child the gift of boundaries.

S: What do you mean, she is laboring with her child?

J: I mean that her relationship now is a labor.

S: She is making up what she didn't do.

J: Yes. In labor, a child learns about boundaries, learns about his or her own energy. I sense that when I am hassling people, I want something back. I want to feel my aliveness. When you come out into the world in a non-labor caesarean, you are still unified with everything. It is an explosion. Your awareness is not confined to your body.

S: That's true for all infants.

J: Maybe even more so for caesareans. In labor you learn how to relate to someone intensely.

S: That is bonding. I hadn't thought about that.

J: One of the positive things about non-labor caesarean is that other people, including the father, get to do some labor.

S: That's more unifying and connecting. Fewer boundaries, more connection and more dependence on other people.

J: Reliance, not dependence. And the mothers can realize they don't have do all the labor.

S: A caesarean birth creates a special experience for the child and for the mother. In vaginal birth, there is a commonality in that they both struggled. But there is also a commonality in caesarean birth that they both experience. I can't say what that commonality is, but I believe it is there. It's just different. The connections are maybe less obvious.

J: Why is all this important? What is the emotion? What is the energy behind our interest in caesarean birth and in a transpersonal perspective? For me, it has a lot to do with caring about the earth, caring about the continuation of the humanity. I have used the metaphor of the tribe or clan. I think of a couple of wonderful caesarean-born people who have helped me. They are like grandmother and grandfather to the caesarean clan. They both had psychotic experiences, were hospitalized, were shocked. I think of the gifts that they gave me in helping me when birth memory was first surfacing into my awareness. I want to spread their knowledge so that people don't have to go through what they went through, or even some of the craziness I went through.

S: We have a new model of being human, and it is worthwhile taking a close look.

J: I see it as requiring that we look at a deeper level. Looking at birth in this way isn't something most people do. It is a step toward a larger, more transpersonal perspective. Knowing a larger reality. Increasing the awareness of a larger connectedness is valuable.

S: It may be what will save us. It also may be that we aren't able to say exactly what are the reasons why we feel all this is important.

Here we commented on how much had changed for both of us since we had shared this material last year.

S: I think what changed for me is that I accepted caesarean birth as a medical procedure that was necessary. When we talked before, I was still saying, "Well, maybe I don't have to do it this way." Then I checked into it and it was clear that it would be dangerous for me to go through vaginal birth. I'm thinking less about the experience and more about the baby. I don't want to endanger that kid at all. Partly because of watching your slides, it doesn't seem so unnatural to me. But I feel like I have no body imagination, even after having the operation, of what it is like to have someone cut you open. Knife cutting, we are taught to stay away from.

J: I think of my inner experience of being a piece of meat. The important thing was the appropriateness of cutting meat. That was a beginning, and I am still integrating it. I think there is a long species memory that being cut is

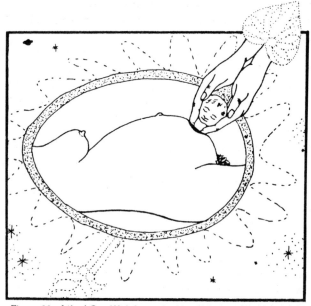

Figure 20—Lifted Out With Love (by Nancy Rosser-Hutchins)

not OK. In order to allow a caesarean birth without resistance, you have to completely turn around that deep conditioning. The picture illustrating my article (*See Figure 20*) shows the wonderful part. The hands lifting out the child with love. But before the hands can get in there, there has to be a cutting. There has to be an invasion.

I change levels of consciousness by being lifted up with love. But before I could get in contact with that, I had to come to terms with the invasion. As long as I resisted the invasion, I felt stuck. If you are willing to allow that radical opening, you can change very fast.

You don't have to go through caesarean birth to be able to do that. It is one of the things that caesarean-born people can teach others. I've seen several non-labor caesarean people who are therapists; and they are incredible. They go right past all kinds of junk and help people go to new levels very easily. Being caesareans, they know how to do it. We need some quick transitions these days.

Interview with Gayle Carlton (*caesarean-born rebirther*)
January 17, 1983.

Gayle Carlton has been a professional rebirther since 1979. She maintains a private practice and also travels nationally teaching about personal transformation and healing through energetics.

As two caesareans who independently had a great deal of experience with the implications of being caesarean, Gayle and I had a lot to share. I was delighted that she not only gave me her thoughts but also did a rebirthing session with me. (See Part II, Chapter 5, September 22, 1982) and shared her knowledge at that level.

G: In my rebirthing practice, I have worked with many people who have had many different types of birth experiences. I have seen that while everyone's birth is different, they are also the same, a journey into the world. I went to see my sister when she was having her baby. I looked at the baby right after she was born. I watched how the nurses treated her and the look on her face. I had a profound and deep feeling of how powerful the birth process is. It is an experience everybody records in their body. I work a lot helping people to overcome the traumatic psychological effects the birth experience can create. Quite a lot of research has been done to validate how the birth experience can scar the personality. It is possible for people to come to certain conclusions about themselves at birth. For example, a common conclusion is, "I am not safe." or "I am not wanted." However, it is not the experience itself that creates the psychological disturbances; they come from the decisions we make about ourselves and the world. Two people with different births, caesarean and vaginal for instance, could come to the the same conclusion. It seems that by magnifying the differences, I have ended up de-emphasizing them.

J: The fear is of getting stuck in the differences when you magnify them. But when you bring more awareness to the differences, they dissolve. You go deeper and find there are no differences. Several people have mentioned to me their fear that I am creating a rigid category for caesarean people.

G: Because of the conclusions and experiences at my birth, I have had to work on my fear and anger about being separate or different. I felt so different because I had a tendency to approach tasks from a different point of view than other people. It would be as though everyone saw the logic of entering from stage right and I wanted to enter from stage left. I have found many caesareans have had the same experience in their lives. They keep thinking that people don't understand them.

One thing in particular I have had to work on was that I have had an extremely hard time letting go of things.

J: What is the fear?

G: It felt like someone was taking away something I needed to be OK.

J: To be OK, or to survive?

G: Both. I noticed in the past, when I let go of a relationship, it felt like something was ripping me into pieces. Letting go of something that I had wanted or that I was under the delusion that I wanted felt like it was being torn out of me. Caesarean births are like being ripped from the womb. When I let go of a business, I had the same feelings in my body. I had to ask myself why I wanted to hold onto the past instead of going forward into the future.

In my birth the separation experience was probably the most traumatic one. When you go through the birth canal, you experience the *process* of separation between yourself and your mother because you feel the walls of the birth canal around your body. There is a several hour long experience of separating through the expansions and contractions. In a caesarean birth it is about a two minute process from in the womb to out. You go from dark to light, from being surrounded in the womb to being in open air about 25 to 30 degrees cooler. You go from being enveloped in your mother's energy to being out of it. It is very abrupt and can also be an emergency situation with lots of tension. So in my life I am always waiting for everything to disappear, especially comfort. There is a feeling of mistrust and insecurity inside me. I noticed that I did not want to know what I wanted in the world because I was afraid it would be taken away from me if I got it. I wasn't prepared for letting go of my mother that fast.

J: You weren't able to maintain any kind of connection.

G: Actually, my mind thought I had killed her.

J: You had that, too!

G: Yes. The anesthetist put her to sleep immediately after my birth. When you sleep, your energy goes somewhere else. Like when you have sex, and the other person falls asleep. That person is not there for you. That is exactly the experience you can have in birth when your mother goes unconscious. You feel abandoned. My mother had a spinal block and was singing through my birth. As soon as I was out they put her under general anesthesia. I had the experience of her being there during the birth, and then she was gone. When I was older and communed with people and became attached to them, I constantly waited for them to leave. No matter how slowly they left, it felt abrupt in my body. I hung on to the past because I couldn't trust the future.

J: In my birth I was feeling the ether and was sinking into it. I fight that feeling now because sinking in means that when I come back, something I depend on will be gone. I may have been out, too, for part of the birth. I think I was on the edge, aware of coming out and yet not aware. I think the bright light brought me back. I feel there is a gap where I don't know what happened. I might have thought I was dying.

G: Yes, I definitely know that at birth I thought they were killing me. In my personal rebirthing experiences a few years ago, I remembered distinctly the fear and panic in my body while thinking I was being killed. The phrase, "They're killing me, they're killing me!" repeated over and over during that rebirth. I actually felt impelled to sit up during the most intense part. It was a year later that I learned the baby is pulled out in a sitting position during a caesarean birth. Then I thought they had killed my mother, I remembered a great deal of fear during those rebirths.

A thought I always remember having, which I believe came from from my birth, was, "I can't do it right." My instinct was to come out of the womb through the birth canal. The doctor denied my instincts in order for me to survive. I have always thought I needed authority, especially men, to protect me and save me from death. Caesareans are known for creating situations in which they have to be rescued.

J: These instincts come from the physical level. A deeper level of you had chosen to be born caesarean.

G: Although I am not certain, I do believe I chose to be born caesarean. However, my physical body, which operates instinctually, probably didn't know that. It knew about going down the canal. My conclusion might be that my instincts would kill me, and somebody else's decision, namely a man's decision, would save me. But being saved by a man led to separation. In my life, when I would choose a way to do something, I usually managed to pull someone in to tell me that it wasn't the right way to do it. Finally, I came to the point where in every single thing I did, there was a thought in the back of my mind that I couldn't do it right.

J: So, what is the way out?

G: One of the ways I did it was through rebirthing. Rebirthing releases energy in your body that has been held around a thought or emotional experience (subconscious material as well as conscious material). The more you think a thought, the more energy it has, the more the evidence in your world seems to prove your thought is true. So, as you release the energy with which you hold on to thoughts, the less your reality seems to prove to you that those thoughts are true.(See Part II, Chapter 5, May 22, 1982 for more on rebirthing.)

J: What is this process of releasing energy?

G: Rebirthing is basically connected and rhythmical breathing. If you keep your breath connected, not holding air in or out, you automatically go through a cycle of energy build-up and release. It clears the energy field around the body and allows acceptance of past emotional material. It allows one to get in touch with who one really is in a very pleasurable way.

J: That build-up and release of energy sounds almost like labor. You begin to allow yourself to follow the wisdom in your body.

G: Yes, rebirthing seems to integrate the mind, body and spirit.

J: So, somehow in this process, you transcend being identified with your limited ego self. You connect with something higher that you call spirit.

G: Exactly!

It seems as though every morning when you wake up, the thoughts that you have from the moment you wake up until you get going are a re-experience of your thoughts at birth.

J: A little rebirth every morning as you come back into your body.

G: Yes, I think that in the back of our minds we are reacting all the time from that physiological map. Most caesareans have a lot of anger and helplessness. One thing that they are angry about is that they fear they must rely on other people in order to survive.

J: What happens when two of these people get together?

G: I find that caesareans have a tendency to be angry, helpless and needy, although this may not be obvious because they may not want other people to know that this is how they feel. If I go into a room, the people who I respond to most I often find out later are caesarean.

I was assisting in a group rebirth. One man was really pushing on his exhale. I knew he was going through a lot of anger. I came up to him and said gently, "Now, relax your exhale." He wouldn't do it. It wasn't that he couldn't do it. I could feel his mind screaming at me, "No, I won't do it. You are not going to tell me how to do it." I realized he was going to have to go through the frustration and anger because he was holding on to it.

Then I was attracted to another man who was struggling in his rebirth. These were the only two people in the room who were being dramatic. I went over to him, touched his head and said gently, "Relax your exhale." I noticed that with both of these people my jaw was clamped down. I was reacting unconsciously in my body to my own birth. The man said, "I can't. I won't." I said that was OK. I had him keep relaxing. He fought me, but because he was willing to communicate it, he was releasing it. Caesareans don't like being told what to do. Then I found out he was a caesarean. I started telling him about caesareans, and he began to relax as he related what I was telling him to his own life. Caesareans may need to get rebirthed more because they have so much fear and resistance. They can only surrender to the energy a little at a time.

When we were done and everyone was sharing, I found out the first man was also caesarean. That angry helplessness is frustrating for anyone to work with. It is not the person. It is that set of thoughts: "I can't do it myself, I can't survive, I'm terrified." All that bound up in a lot of anger: "I can't get what I want. No one can help me."

J: What is helping you move beyond that yourself?

G: Taking responsibility for my thoughts, first of all, then becoming aware of how my thoughts have produced repetitive patterns of behavior and circumstance in my life. Being willing to surrender was one of the biggest things I had to learn. I had thick walls up which kept out a lot of love and appreciation from others. Fortunately, the people in the rebirthing business who have been my teachers have assisted me in a way that made me feel safe in surrendering. Learning that there is no separation was valuable, difficult and fairly recent. That's also needed by people who aren't caesarean.

J: These are universal processes we all go through, but there are different styles. It is the same end point, but the path you take may be a little different.

G: Yes, I agree.

I realize how much caesarean thought patterns can be different from those of the vaginally born when I am with another caesarean. My life experience is understood much more by a caesarean. There has been a sense of relief, that I am not crazy. It is a mutual validation. I have had confrontations with people who were vaginally born who had absolutely no understanding of what I was talking about. I wasn't talking about caesarean birth; I was trying to explain the way I was perceiving something. They just couldn't understand me. I would go away feeling invalidated. Then I would say exactly the same thing to caesareans, and they would say, "I know exactly what you mean." I can find a caesarean in a group. Some psychic sense pulls me in.

J: I see that between two caesareans there might be two poles, real attraction or intense dislike.

G: Yes. And I think it is important for caesareans to have a book that will validate their life experience and raise their self-esteem. It is important in a world where almost 20 percent of the births are caesarean.

J: I think there is also a sense of pioneering and leadership among caesareans. It is the flip side of the helplessness. A certain strength comes from living outside the mainstream. You get your own resources going, and when you get past the separateness, you find you have a lot of strength. Caesarean birth is an ideal structure for allowing something new to come through into the world. It sets aside some deep patterns that have been common to all human culture. We begin to realize that we don't have to do some things the way people have been doing them for thousands of years.

G: Yes, looking at the positive side of the surgical birth is great! One of the ways that has been important in healing the negative conclusions I made from my birth was seeing how much support I got at my birth. I had a mother who was willing to have my body, a doctor to do the surgery, nurses to take care of me, and a wonderful mother to serve me in infancy until I could function on my own. It was wonderful to let go of my perception that I was a helpless victim and to see how powerful it is to relax and have people come in and take care of me. I didn't struggle in the birth at all.

J: You didn't struggle when they were getting the breathing going?

G: I did when they were poking me to get me breathing. Hospital procedure at that time was to cut the umbilical cord quickly and stimulate the baby to cry immediately. This forces the infant to gasp for air.

I tell people if they want to know what it was like to be born caesarean to imagine that one night they are sound asleep and totally relaxed. Then four people charge into the room, open the drapes, turn on the lights, make a lot of noise, pull the covers off, grab you by the feet, hang you upside down, tell you to breathe, put you back down and rub you roughly. Your thoughts would be, "Who are these people? What are they doing? Are they trying to kill me?"

J: It is a good analogy. I wish people would make up a similar story for vaginal birth, because that's a mystery to me.

G: I think vaginal births are like earthquakes. I'd like to know what happens in the mind when you are in the uterus and labor starts. According to research, the baby starts labor; an enzyme is secreted. Imagine what it must be like to have your whole body squeezed at once. When I rebirth vaginally-born people and they go into contractions, they tighten all their muscles. They'll be totally relaxed and breathing and then their body goes into a contraction. They literally re-experience what it felt like to be squeezed that tightly.

><><><><><><><><><><><><><><><><><><

Conversation with Anne Stine (*caesarean-born therapist*)
January 18, 1983.

Anne Stine is a transpersonal counselor in private practice in Volcano, California. She specializes in death and dying and is on the board and staff of Hospice of Amador.

Sharing with Anne, both in conversation and by letter, was a good completion. Her experience as a caesarean affirmed mine. She then reminded me of the process of transcending attachment to birth learning and going on to something higher.

J: Tell me about re-experiencing your birth.
A: I did that some years back. I checked it out with my mother before she died. It was all true as far as she was concerned, which was exciting. What I experienced was that I wasn't ready to be born. I felt like I was taken before my time and against my will somewhat. I would say the overall theme after that, if there is any relationship between my birth and my life experiences, was that I have had a great deal of trouble, not so much in taking initiative, as in following through on it. I feel I don't have to do it myself. I've worked a lot on the issues of dependency and demands. But I am not convinced this is unique to caesarean-born people.
J: I am not saying it is unique. But it may be emphasized. I see the map I am constructing as something people will use as a tool, as a way of getting perspective on and transcending some of the patterns caesarean have.
A: Transcendence may or may not be related to being caesarean. I find that not only the ability to go into higher states of consciousness, but also the belief and knowledge that these states exist, has always been a part of me. When I look at this through the lens of birth, it is like a whole part of the birthing process was missing. I didn't experience a resistance. I don't like resistance.
J: That sounds like what other caesareans say, especially about the connection to higher states of consciousness. And it is valuable to teach people that they don't have to go through all the struggle, the labor.
A: When I am involved with groups, there often seems to me to be a tremendous amount of time and energy wasted that I have little tolerance for.

What have you found out about the issue of boundaries?
J: For caesareans, one of the problems in appreciating our easy access to higher consciousness is that we don't know boundaries well enough to be able to know that this expanded awareness is something special. There are difficulties also with not knowing what are someone else's feelings and what are mine, taking on whatever is around, or else shoving everyone away. Not knowing the middle ground, how to take on a little bit and then back off. It is all or nothing.

A: One of the things I have gotten in touch with recently is anger. I get angry when I let someone intrude upon me. I can come across as someone who can easily be walked upon. I violate myself over and over by letting people intrude. I get angry, but I don't express the anger. Eventually it comes out sideways rather than directly.

It has precipitated me into doing radical and rebellious things with my life. Making sudden abrupt changes.

J: Deep down you didn't believe you could change, so you ended up doing it over and over.

A: My mother and I battled each other a lot. Only by comparison with friends over the years have I seen how cruel and violent it was. We didn't physically hurt each other, but I said things and took actions in order to extricate myself. I think of your dream of killing your mother.

J: One of the things that I think will help caesarean-born people is to see that struggle as labor. Labor, the creation of boundaries, has to happen sometime, and not much of it happened at birth. So you and your mother had to labor with each other. If the mother knows she is laboring with the child, there will be a lot less negative judgment.

A: I like that. We threw such judgment and criticism around at each other. We weren't able to leave each other alone until she knew she was going to die. At that point it was, "Either shit or get off the pot." We both grew up. I could accept her, and she could accept me.

J: It helped me in my relationship with my mother when I saw it as labor. I was able to let go of a lot of judgment. I thought, "Oh, we have been laboring with each other."

A: (looking at the picture of my Pink Teddy, with a zippered stomach *See Figure 1*)I have one, too! It is a brown cat.

J: That is going to amaze people when I show a picture of the two of them in my slide show, and say, "Here are the favorite toys of a couple of caesarean-born people.

A: All the hair rubbed off and kissed, rips sewn up.

J: For me it was the beginning of healing the wound.

March 4, 1983

Dear Jane,

I want to add one more experience which has come up recently which I feel is related to my birth.

Although the "victim" experience is common to everyone, there is a quality to it which I feel relates to the apparent absence of choice at the time of caesarean birth, and which I have experienced as an absence of will. This occurs when I am close to true creative action and reads something like, "I don't want to come out." At its most intense, it has felt like a total absence of initiative, combined with suffocation.

At the same time there is an expectation that I will be taken care of. (Things have, in fact, always turned out in a most wonderful and, in a sense, easy fashion.) However, the paradox here is a lack of trust in the overall intelligence of the universe, i.e. doubting that I truly am in God's care. This has created a fear of letting go, although I also know that higher, or altered states of consciousness are accessible to me. This easy access can be terrifying when accompanied by a lack of trust and initiative. Then I don't let go to the experience of the higher state, and I don't know what is real, don't know what to trust. When feeling victim, lacking trust and will power, and fearing letting go all converge, it becomes "being stuck." The fear is that I will always be like that.

With the caesarean birth patterns in my consciousness, my commitment over the years has been to find my true experience in the moment, regardless of how it looks. If, as Grof outlines, certain universal patterns of creativity and approaching life are found in the stages of vaginal birth, and if we caesareans are missing those, then we are challenged to find alternative, new patterns of creativity that are compatible with our birth process. Then the split between victim and aggressor gives way and the creator emerges.

Good luck, and
with love,
Anne

March 14, 1983

Yesterday I called Anne. She said that after writing the letter, she'd come to an even deeper understanding of the pattern of feeling "not ready," of being a victim.

She said, "Having missed 'normal birth' doesn't mean I have to make it up. There is a wholeness and perfection right now. The feeling of being a victim comes from the belief in having missed something, feeling I have to make myself ready."

She said she'd just recently experienced being totally ready to be born and had understood that the "not ready" was simply material to work with in this lifetime, a metaphor. She learned that when one is ready, birth can be effortless. It does not have to be hard to come out; it does not have to be difficult to go into new states of consciousness.

Part IV

The Journey in Perspective
And The Path Ahead

May 1984

Now the question is, what do we do with all this? Each of us will have our own answer.

It has been more than ten years since I began to conceptualize my experience in terms of being born caesarean. Now it is time for me to let go of this particular structure. It is important for me to move on. I am beginning to look at this grand transpersonal territory to which I have been led. The caesarean material has been my vehicle. One of my hopes is that pieces of this book will be useful to you in the creation of your own way of moving into this larger perspective on what it is to be human.

There is more to being human than our daily routine in the ordinary world. Something eternal comes in with us through birth. And something eternal leaves through the other gateway, through our death. This something is not the physical body or the ordinary mind. The connection to that larger existence in the realm before birth and after death sheds a different light on what it is to be a human. It doesn't matter what the particulars of your birth were. The particulars of being born caesarean were simply my vehicle to reach some understanding of the greater.

Some of what this book evoked in you may have delighted you, and some may have horrified you. But as you have seen in my accounts, fear can be a guide. Fear often points to a demon and it is very likely that this demon hides some treasure. I trust you will take whatever is evoked and explore it. You have your own resources, most importantly the inner part of you that knows the way for you to go.

On the other hand, you may feel that what you have read is far-fetched and makes a big deal about nothing. Sometimes I feel that way, too. Simply set those parts aside and know they are not for you. The process of choosing what to leave in the book and what to take out of the book has been difficult. At times I have probably said too much for some of you and too little for others.

The comparison between caesarean birth and vaginal birth can teach us a great deal. Until about 100 years ago the vast majority of people were born vaginally. "Birth" meant "vaginal birth." A metaphor that I use for this is: If the only kind of fruit we knew were apples, we probably wouldn't have two words. We'd have one word that meant "fruit-apple." Then a banana appears, and our sense of what fruit is expands. It becomes more abstract and is not tied to the particulars of either form of fruit, apple or banana. During the whole history of the human race part of being human was the journey down the birth canal. Now, an increasingly large percentage of humans are born caesarean; they don't go down the birth canal. Bananas have joined the apples (*See Figure 21*). We have an opportunity to become aware of a deeper level of humanness that transcends both kinds of birth learning, the patterns learned in caesarean birth and the patterns learned in vaginal birth.

Figure 21a—Apples   Figure 21b—Apples and Banana

Looking at the concepts I used along the way—boundaries, labor, separateness/union, intrusion/interruption, dependence, nourishment—I find I can say that my birth played a major part in shaping my concepts of space—identity, separation, who and what I am—and of time—how I move, change and relate to others. Something as basic as one's experience of space and time deserves to be called a world view. If, as my preliminary sharings with other caesarean-born people indicate, this world view is similar to that of other caesareans, it is meaningful to speak of it as a caesarean world view. But the question is not one of whether this caesarean world view exists, but of how useful this idea is to caesareans and to non-caesareans.

After all, who really knows what it is like to "be caesarean." I am not just caesarean. I am also female, white, forty-two, raised in New England and living in California in 1984. What I have done is to show what happened for me during the ten years that I used "caesarean born" as a lens through which to look at the world and at myself.

I would be most interested in hearing what other people experience while using this lens. I have, in part, been defining "caesarean born," at least the psychological and spiritual aspects of it. Others will extend, refine and change the definition. They will reshape the lens from the inside, through their experience.

The lens also can be reshaped from the outside through scientific studies of the behavior and attitudes of caesarean-born people. Both kinds of re-definition are needed and useful. They are complementary.

October 2, 1984

There is a final jewel to share. In November 1983, I was a participant in a shamanism workshop led by Michael Harner, an anthropologist internationally recognized for his scholarly work on the shamanic cultures of the world and for his teaching of the methods of shamanism.

—137—

In his workshop he spoke of the shaman's role as "psychopomp," as conductor of the souls of recently dead people into the worlds beyond. In the shamanic journeys described below, trance journeys into a non-ordinary reality, I became aware of the possibility of a shaman acting as a psychopomp-in-reverse, as a conductor of souls from the other worlds into this one at birth.

In the first journey, one done with the intention of getting information from "ancestors" about rituals for healing and for transformation, I find a group of caesarean-born people who have recently died. They are very glad to see me. They tell me about the abruptness of caesarean birth, about never having really inhabited their bodies. They hope I am doing better. I say I am, with lots of help. They are my "ancestors!"

I become aware that part of me has always been in touch with the light of spirit, and that I usually make a great effort to deny it and to be in "ordinary" reality. I get a strong message from these "ancestors" that my role in life is to teach about earth, body, heartbeat, breathing, etc. *with* awareness of light. Seeing "body" as an extraordinary state of consciousness.

In a second journey on the same day, I go again to my caesarean friends who are sitting around a fire. They have been discussing my previous visit and are glad to see me again. I ask them for ways to ease the transition of caesarean birth; I expect them to give me a ritual or technique.

They tell me all that is necessary is to have someone unify in consciousness, spiritually, with the babies, stay with them and help them affirm their decisions to incarnate. The person should stay unified with the baby until he or she opens his or her eyes, breathes easily and clearly agrees to being in a body. All other techniques are secondary. It is OK to use whatever seems appropriate at the moment.

I ask, "Is that all there is to it?" The caesareans laugh and say, "What did you expect, labor or something?" We howl with laughter and dance around the fire.

After these journeys I wanted to learn all I could about the traditional shaman's ways in order to begin to bring this new vision of caesarean birth into reality. I joined Michael's month-long tutorial in shamanism at Esalen in January 1984. Since then shamanism, especially work on going easily back and forth between realities, has become an increasingly large part of my life.

My friend Rowena Pattee has been a fellow traveler in shamanic adventuring. This morning we sat together meditating, journeying into other realities, and speaking of our experiences.

My left shoulder hurt. I became aware of intense fear. Her presence, and her inner union with me, helped me to stay with it and to bring in the inner light, which initially intensified the pain. Then came awareness of hurt and anger, then back to birth. Again I felt all the pain and the sense of being ineptly and abruptly unfolded and dragged out. Then came a flash of insight.

A caesarean birth does not have to be painful and fragmenting. Mine was because the people delivering me were unaware of what birth really is. I was dulled by the anesthesia. I was not greeted or recognized as the being of light I am. I contracted and hid. I have been hiding ever since. I even forgot I was hiding and believed I was only the small contracted being I had become.

My journey, chronicled in this book, is the story of uncovering and unfolding, of re-discovering who I really am. I am coming home to the being of light who has been trying to shine out all this time.

The violent contracting and the subsequent long journey of healing is not necessary if the person doing the caesarean is fully conscious and trained in medical techniques *and* the subtle spiritual realms. The doctor-shaman needs to unify with the spirit of the child and allow not just medical training but also spiritual wisdom and the ways of the heart to inform his or her hands. Then the birth can be like the gentle opening of a lotus flower rising up to receive the light of the sun.

I now know this is possible. The instinctual mother-wisdom of how to give birth, literally, as a gift to the child, is being extended. It is no longer confined, semi-conscious, to the lower part of the body of Woman. It is being made conscious in the hands, mind and heart of Human, in both males and females.

The road to being able to practice this in caesarean deliveries may be long and hard. But we know the direction to go.

October 30, 1984

In the past few weeks Rowena has helped me experience and more fully release my birth-memory demons. It has been like walking through fire together. Today I saw how I was still clinging to her sheltering presence. I realized she can't give me what I need. I remembered the painting on the cover of this book and realized the person is walking through the fire *alone*. I saw that was what I need to do. I wondered if the intense fear of "walking through fire" alone is a birth memory. I may have already done it!

Even with the help of a doctor-shaman, there is a moment when the person being born "walks through the fire" totally alone. This is the initiation, the moment of birth, of death and rebirth. It is the moment when an individual human comes into being in physical form. And this experience of utter separateness is, paradoxically, the beginning of conscious awareness of union with the cosmos.

Bibliography

Tools for Journeying:

Campbell, Joseph, *Hero With a Thousand Faces,* Cleveland, World Publishing, 1965.

> A classic work relating the journey of heroes of many mythologies to the spiritual or inner journey.

Esalen Catalog, published three times per year. Write or call Esalen Institute, Big Sur, CA 93920. Tel. (408) 667-2335.

> Workshops and seminars at Esalen, including many similar to those mentioned in this book.

Harner, Michael, *The Way of the Shaman,* New York, Bantam, 1982.

> Universal shamanic techniques refined out of the traditions of many cultures. Ways of journeying into non-ordinary reality for power and healing.

Laut, Phil, and Jim Leonard, *Rebirthing,* Hollywood, Trinity Publications, 1983.

> An introduction to rebirthing as a technique for releasing fixed patterns of consciousness.

Metzner, Ralph, *Opening to Inner Light: Transformation of Human Nature and Consciousness,* Los Angeles, Tarcher, forthcoming.

> Metaphors of transformation from nature and from mythology. Tools for relating different levels of reality.

Metzner, Ralph, *Maps of Consciousness,* New York, Collier-Macmillan, 1971.

> Introductions to Tarot, I Ching, Astrology, Alchemy and other maps. The last chapter is a good introduction to light-fire meditation techniques.

Perinatal Psychology (birth psychology):

Feher, Leslie, *The Psychology of Birth*, New York, Continuum, 1980.

> Good descriptions of personality traits associated with different kinds of birth. Interpretations are limited by its author's Freudian, mechanistic conceptual framework.

Grof, Stanislav, *Beyond the Brain: Birth, Death, and Transcendence in Psychotherapy*, Albany, New York, State University of New York Press, 1985.

> A new model of the human psyche that encompasses the recollective biographical, the perinatal and the transpersonal realms of experience. His newest, most comprehensive book.

Grof, Stanislav, *Realms of the Human Unconscious*, New York, Dutton, 1976.

> A pioneering work that maps the progressively deeper layers of the psyche: personal history, perinatal experience and the transpersonal. Includes a detailed map of the relation between a person's vaginal birth experience and their later personality traits.

Janov, Arthur, *Imprints: The Lifelong Effects of the Birth Experience*, New York, Coward-McCann, 1983.

> Extensive material on the reliving of birth and the release of behavior unconsciously based on birth memory. Written within the framework of primal therapy. Does not have a spiritual perspective.

Verny, Thomas, *The Secret Life of the Unborn Child*, New York, Dell, 1982.

> Descriptions of accurate, documented *pre*-natal memories beside which birth memory looks quite matter of course.

Transpersonal Psychology:

Journal of Transpersonal Psychology, published by Transpersonal Institute, Box 3049, Stanford, CA 94305.

Vaughan, Frances, and Roger Walsh, eds., *Beyond Ego*, Los Angeles, J.P. Tarcher, 1980.

> A good introductory compilation of writings in transpersonal psychology.

Armstrong, Thomas, *The Radiant Child*, Wheaton, Ill., Quest Books, 1985.

> Children's transpersonal and mystical experiences from pre-birth through adolescence. A practical guide for parents, teachers, and child-therapists.

Medical Aspects of Caesarean Birth:

Affonso, Dyanne, *The Impact of Caesarean Birth,* Philadelphia, F.A. Davis, 1981.

> Written for medical professionals, but easily readable by others. Covers in detail the medical techniques of caesarean birth and also some of the psychology of the mother's experience.

Donovan, Bonnie, *The Caesarean Birth Experience,* Boston, Beacon Press, 1977.

Mayer, Linda, *The Caesrean (R)evolution,* Edmonds, WA, Chas. Franklin Press, 1979.

> Guides to caesarean birth's medical aspects and to the mother's experience. Handbooks for parents.

Marieskind, Helen, *An Evaluation of Caesarean Section in the United States,* Washington D.C., Dept. of HEW, 1979.

> Statistics on caesarean birth and discussion of policy regarding caesarean birth.

Pundel, J.P., *Histoire de L'Operation Cesarienne,* Brussels, Presses Academiques Europiennes, 1969.

> An excellent comprehensive history of caesarean birth. Many illustrations, good sections on mythlogy and legend. In French, but worth looking at even if just for the illustrations.

Science—The New Physics:

Capra, Fritjof, The Tao of Physics, Berkeley, Shambala, 1975.

Zukav, Gary, *The Dancing Wu Li Masters,* New York, Morrow, 1979.

> Two books that, in non-technical language, show the way through the mechanistic Newtonian physics that is the basis for what most people think of as science, and on to the more recent quantum physics and relativity theories that seem to parallel both ancient mystical systems and modern theories of consciousness.

Dossey, Larry, M.D., *Space, Time, and Medicine,* Boulder, Shambala, 1982.

> The application of the concepts of the new physics to social science and medicine. Relating these strange new realities to everyday experience.

An Additional Resource: The Pre and Perinatal Psychology Association of North America, 93 Harbord Street, Toronto, Ontario, Canada, N5S 1G4, publishes the proceedings of its international congresses and can give international referrals to medical birth professionals and to researchers and practitioners of prenatal and perinatal psychology.

About the Author

Jane Butterfield English was born in Boston in 1942 and grew up in an old farmhouse and in the woods north of Boston. She has a Ph.D. from the University of Wisconsin in sub-atomic particle physics. The best known of the four books she has illustrated with her black and white photographs of nature is a translation of Lao Tsu's *Tao Te Ching*. Ten years of psychological and spiritual self-exploration inspired her to write *Different Doorway* and furthered her interest in meditation and shamanic practices as tools for personal growth and for contributing to the healing of the immense problems that face our planet.